White House Doctor

White House Doctor

T. Burton Smith, M.D.
with
Carter Henderson

MADISON BOOKS
Lanham • New York • London

Published by Madison Books
4720 Boston Way
Lanham, Maryland 20706

Distributed by National Book Network

The paper used in this publication meets the minimum
requirements of American National Standard for
Information Sciences—Permanence of Paper for
Printed Library Materials, ANSI Z39.48–1984. ∞™
Manufactured in the United States of America.

Library of Congress Cataloging-in-Publication Data

Smith, T. Burton.
White House doctor / T. Burton Smith with Carter
Henderson.
p.   cm.
1. Reagan, Ronald—Health.   2. Bush, George,
1924–   —Health.   3. Smith, T. Burton.
4. Physicians—United States—Biography.
I. Henderson, Carter F.   II. Title.
E877.2.S66   1992
973.927'0922—dc20   92–31506 CIP

ISBN 0–8191–8625–2 (cloth : alk. paper)

To
Kit
for her indefatigable spirit
and to my own
First Family
for their unfailing support

Contents

Preface

I am a physician and surgeon and was fortunate to have established a medical relationship, over the past twenty-five years, with Ronald Reagan.

As I reminisce about those experiences, it becomes obvious that there were many medical events along the path for both President and Mrs. Reagan. Each was properly diagnosed, the problem was met head-on, the correct course of action was planned, all culminated in definitive surgery, and to date, all have reached a successful conclusion. Had this not been true, the course of history would no doubt have been changed as we know it today.

Much credit is due to the state of the art of medicine and surgery as carried out in the United States of America today. Equal credit must also be given to the courage, bravado, and positive attitude of the patient . . . to this latter point, President and Mrs. Reagan have been outstanding role models and, I am certain, have been helpful to people the world over. The good that they have done, medically, is inestimable.

The fallout of medical information was worldwide and covered a variety of medical topics. The public, therefore, was informed about diagnostic methods in a descriptive and graphic manner. Authorities in their respective fields pontificated on the problem at hand, the possible treatment options, and the anticipated outcome. Because of the popularity of the then First Family, media coverage was exceptionally widespread resulting in the dissemination of a wide range of knowledge not possible by any other modality.

To date, the public, by virtue of close media coverage, obtained all the medical information that was necessary for a full disclosure of medical events during my White House years.

The chronology of this book follows the documentation laid down in the media reports and the ten or more books written to date covering recollections for the period under discussion.

I thought Washington, D.C., was a wonderful and exciting place to live and work. I found the White House complex to be historical and immaculate, and I never tired of being there. I found the people surrounding the president to be loyal, bright, attractive, and anxious to please (perhaps too anxious to please . . . time will tell.) President and Mrs. Reagan did much to make us feel at home in our new and different surroundings.

Finally, I should like to thank President and Mrs. Ronald Reagan for allowing me to share in this unique experience. I shall be eternally grateful.

There is a great deal more to the presidency than politics . . .

T B S

Acknowledgments

A book of this type does not just happen. There must be a unique experience involving engaging personalities during an interesting period of history. My appointment as Physician to President Ronald Reagan during the Reagan administration adequately fulfilled these requirements.

Originally, I had planned to write a chronicle, to be given to our four children and ten grandchildren. This was changed to a book form when my medical colleagues at Saint John's Hospital told me their patients had been helped by observing how President Reagan dealt with his own medical problems. I realized there was a message here that should be told and that, I hope, will be helpful to many people. To the Reagans, my family, and my medical friends, thank you for providing this concept.

I must thank the people of the White House Medical Unit for support, advice, and attention to details that made my time at the White House as stress-free as possible. Chief of Staff Donald Regan deserves thanks in overriding the "TTWWADI" (that's the way we've always done it) mentality when I presented innovative medical changes. Jumping into a totally new and different environment was softened by the gentle direction and sound advice of many helpful experts among the staff: these professionals have my gratitude for not letting me fall too hard or too far. The illustrations were taken by gifted White House photographers and became part of my private collection that graphically chronicled the events.

When it came to getting the bits of data together and organizing them into book form, Carter Henderson was the man. Many times I gave up on the project but was guided back on track by Carter's gentle persuasion. Without him there would be no book.

Medical ethics, dealing with doctor-patient relationships, is a delicate matter. The media's handling of the "public's-right-to-know" has made many of these concerns moot for most public figures, but I still did not want to compromise the Reagans' trust. I was grateful to have the manuscript read by Charles Plows, M.D., formerly head of the Ethics Committee of the American Medical Association, who saw no reason to make changes.

When it came time for editing and matters-of-fact, many came to my aid and were generous with their time and advice. Medical details were edited by several experts: Donald Wagner, M.D., surgeon; Richard Taw, M.D., cardiologist; and Harry Miller, M.D., urologist. Of great help on White House matters were Dale Petrosky, formerly with the press office, and Burton Lee III, M.D., the present White House Physician. Sensitive Secret Service matters were revised by Ray Shaddick, and the Twenty-fifth Amendment assessment was capably reviewed by Dr. Kenneth Thompson of the Miller Center for Presidential Affairs in Virginia.

Hours of revising, rewriting, and proofing became a family affair. Kit, who knew what I was attempting to relate, read miles of word processor printouts; Sandy, an English major, corrected grammar and spelling; and Deanne, a judge, advised on content and pace. All this was returned to Carter, who wrote it all over again.

Finally, I am grateful to Madison Books for having faith in making the manuscript into a book and to my editor, Jennifer Smith, for steering this volume through the publication maze.

Introduction

Just before I left the White House as personal physician to President Ronald Reagan and Vice President George Bush, President Reagan appointed me to the Board of Regents of the Uniformed Services University of the Health Sciences in Bethesda, Maryland, a short subway ride from Capitol Hill. The medical school trains students to become Army, Navy, Air Force, and Public Health Service doctors, and several times a year I fly to Washington from my home in Los Angeles to attend Regents meetings in Bethesda, whose complex of medical facilities is rich in the history of White House doctors and their patients from George Washington to George Bush.

It was at a meeting on presidential illness at the Uniformed Services University that I first met George Bush's White House physician, Dr. Burton J. Lee, III, who came to Washington from a distinguished career as a specialist in cancers of the lymph system at Manhattan's Memorial Sloan-Kettering Cancer Center. Dr. Lee and I have had some fascinating conversations about our very different approaches to safeguarding the president's health in the Bush and Reagan White Houses.

I was never more than minutes away from President Reagan's side, whereas Dr. Lee often assigns another White House doctor to accompany the president if Mr. Bush's schedule suddenly changes, and he has an important outside commitment he feels he cannot break. Dr. Lee was by President Bush's side on January 8, 1992, however, when he collapsed from a bout of intestinal flu at a state dinner in Tokyo given for him by Japanese Prime Minister Kiichi Miyazawa.

A short stroll from the Uniformed Services School is the National Naval Medical Center, which has cared for U.S. presidents going back to Franklin D. Roosevelt, who helped design it. The autopsy on Presi-

dent John F. Kennedy was performed there the night of his assassination in Dallas. I've accompanied President Reagan on countless ten-
minute helicopter rides from the White House to the hospital for
everything from his annual physical checkups to major surgery. And
President Bush was flown there on May 4, 1991, after suffering a
rapid, irregular beating of his heart—known as atrial fibrillation—
while jogging at Camp David, the presidential retreat in the Maryland
mountains.

A few steps from the Naval Hospital is the National Library of
Medicine, whose 3.5 million volumes dating back to the eleventh
century make it the largest medical research library in the world. Even
a casual search of the library's collection, however, reveals something
which surprised me and encouraged me to write this book.

What the National Library of Medicine makes abundantly clear is
that relatively little has been written about the medical care of presidents of the United States. Articles in medical journals are most
common, although relatively few in number, and books are rarer still.

One president whose medical history has survived in considerable
detail is George Washington's. The Father of Our Country was a
towering figure in his own time, and his letters, diaries, and other
health-related memorabilia were preserved in what amounted to a
sacred trust.

Reading how Washington's doctors looked after him is to understand
the revolution that has taken place in medicine since the 1700s.
Doctors back then believed that disease was caused by an imbalance
in the body's "four humors," consisting of "blood, phlegm, yellow bile,
and black bile." Today's doctors believe that each disease has a specific
cause and a specific cure.

The only book I found that was actually written by a president's
doctor is *White House Physician,* by Admiral Ross T. McIntire, M.D.,
who looked after Franklin D. Roosevelt. Dr. McIntire's book was
published in 1946, when White House physicians had not yet begun
the practice of disclosing the most intimate details of their patient's
condition; that practice began with the late Dr. Howard Snyder's press
briefings following President Dwight D. Eisenhower's near-fatal heart
attack on September 24, 1955. I've included in this book an unpublished account sent to me by Dr. Snyder's son, in which his father
recounts how he had President Eisenhower's wife, Mamie, "wrap
herself around him in bed" to calm his fears and increase his chances
of surviving his heart attack.

What I've attempted to do in this book is describe how today's White

House doctors go about caring for the president of the United States. Each of us approaches the job differently, influenced as we are by our own medical training and beliefs, our personal relationship with the president, and the need to constantly monitor his crushing workload for signs that it's damaging his health.

The medical care which surrounds the president of the United States is in a class by itself. No other world leader has anything like it, a fact I learned firsthand in meetings with physicians to heads of state from Egypt to the Soviet Union. This book tells that story for the first time.

Chapter One

"The President Has Been Shot"

I was flying from Los Angeles to Washington, D.C., on March 30, 1981, to attend a medical meeting, and had arranged to stop by the White House to say hello to President Ronald Reagan, who had been a patient of mine for fifteen years. An hour out of St. Louis, enroute to Washington's National Airport, the pilot's voice came over the intercom telling us President Reagan had been shot. I looked in disbelief at my wife, Kathleen, who was seated next to me. Who would want to shoot President Ronald Reagan? He had been in office less than three months, and as far as I knew had no enemies. Perhaps there was some mistake. Maybe I had dozed off and had dreamed it. But it was true, and for the next few minutes we sat helplessly waiting for the captain's next report over the passenger intercom.

The stewardess stopped by to chat, and I told her the irony of it all was that we had a date to see the president in the White House Oval Office the next morning at 11 A.M. I guess I felt I had to prove my point because I showed her my confirmation letter, and she asked if she could take it up to the cockpit to show the captain. He returned and said that the latest reports indicated that President Reagan was in surgery, and that our flight had been diverted away from Washington to Tennessee in case the assassination attempt was part of a larger conspiracy.

It wasn't until around 11 P.M. that night that we were directed to land at National Airport in Washington. During the spectacular approach along the Potomac River, I couldn't help looking at the city lights and wondering what was going on down there. From the air it appeared quiet, clean and peaceful, but I knew very well there was great turmoil, bewilderment, and confusion in the nation's capital. We were now opposite the White House, and as I looked out the window

1

to my left it reminded me of an illuminated birthday cake—quiet, dignified and serene. But I knew that despite the outward calmness, inside there was hushed apprehension as the cabinet and staff waited for some word.

As we taxied up to the ramp, National Airport seemed unusually quiet. People moved slowly, talked in hushed tones, or were clustered in small groups over portable radios listening to the latest news reports on President Reagan's condition.

I felt we couldn't be of any help to the president in Washington, so we caught the last shuttle to historic Williamsburg, Virginia, staying overnight in the quiet of the Williamsburg Inn, where we could gather our thoughts. The next morning I placed a call through the White House switchboard to President Reagan's personal physician, Dr. Daniel A. Ruge. I told him I was staying in nearby Williamsburg, and was ready to help if needed. Dr. Ruge said everything was fine, but telephoned me three days later to say President Reagan wanted to see me.

Dr. Ruge met me at the George Washington University Hospital, where President Reagan had been rushed after being hit by one of six bullets fired by twenty-five-year-old John Hinkley, Jr., who had been waiting for him as he left the Washington Hilton Hotel following a speech to a labor convention. The president had undergone emergency surgery to stop massive bleeding in his chest cavity, replace 3.7 quarts of lost blood, and remove a bullet lodged in his lung an inch away from his heart.

Dr. Ruge gave me a lapel identification pin, and a Secret Service agent escorted us to a secured manned elevator, which took us up to the president's floor in the hospital's South Wing. It had been entirely closed off, as had the streets surrounding the hospital as a precaution against sharpshooters. We were then led through a series of barriers guarded by the White House Presidential Protective Detail, across floors covered with thick communications cables, and into an anteroom of the presidential suite. I was told to wait there until President Reagan, dressed in pajamas, bathrobe, and slippers, had finished walking up and down the corridor a few times with Mrs. Reagan.

A Filipino steward from the White House mess, smartly dressed in gray slacks and a blue blazer with the presidential seal on his left breast pocket, offered me a cup of coffee. As I waited for the president and Mrs. Reagan to enter the room, I thought about what I was going to say to him, and if I should shake hands with her, kiss her on the cheek, or curtsy now that she was the First Lady of the land.

The president finally finished his walk, and as he entered the room he was coughing a bit, so I didn't encourage him to talk. As it turned out, I didn't need to, because the moment he spotted me he said, "Damn you West Coast doctors! You didn't warn me about lead poisoning when I moved here to Washington." The president was clearly uncomfortable talking, so we chatted for just a few more minutes. I told the president I thought he looked great, that I'd be keeping an eye on his progress, and to call me if I could be useful. As I left, I felt Mrs. Reagan had been relieved to see me; a familiar face from California bringing what I hoped was a sense of calm to this terrible time in her life, just a few weeks after moving into the White House.

Dr. Ruge and I left the hospital through a small rear door opening onto a block-long section of I Street, which had been cordoned off by Washington, D.C. police. Across the street were dozens of reporters, photographers, and television people who went on full alert when they spotted us. TV cameras whirred, and hours later friends of mine on the West Coast said they were surprised to have seen what they thought was me on the evening news since they didn't even know I was in Washington.

Dr. Ruge got into a dark blue White House Chrysler LeBaron waiting for us by the curb, but I decided to walk back to my hotel. I had taken only a few steps when an attractive young television newswoman walked up and asked me who I was, if I'd seen President Reagan, and, if so, how I thought he looked. I told her I was an old friend of the president's from the West Coast and that I thought he looked great. Little did I realize, as I got over the shock of my first encounter with Washington reporters, that in less than four years I'd be regularly dealing with them as President Reagan's White House physician.

Invitation from the President

Ronald Reagan is an immensely likable man, which is why I left my home, friends, and medical practice in Los Angeles to be with him in Washington. Apparently a lot of people agreed with me because, according to a *New York Times*/CBS News Poll, 68 percent of the American people approved of Ronald Reagan's overall job performance during his eight years in the White House—the highest rating given any president at the end of his term since World War II.

I had a successful, six-figure practice in Los Angeles as a surgeon specializing in urology, which involves the urinary and genital functions and organs. I had been building this practice for more than thirty-five years when I gave it up to serve President Reagan for $72,300 a year. "Poor Burton," said a dentist friend of mine, named Smokey Martin, during a toast-and-roast dinner at the Santa Monica Beach Club in California celebrating my seventieth birthday, "he was doing so well and now he's just another government doctor with only one patient."

What helped ease the transition from my sprawling home in an avocado grove in the Brentwood section of Los Angeles to a two-bedroom flat in Washington's Watergate apartment complex was that I could leave my patients under the able care of my associate Dr. Thomas Mitchell. I was also relieved that I no longer had to look after patients the way medicine is practiced today. I had been a successful doctor for a long time with a good track record. Yet like all doctors in recent years, I had to constantly contend with peer review groups looking over my shoulder, third-party payers such as Blue Cross intervening in what I thought was best for my patients, and secretaries telling me, "You can't admit that patient," or "Hey, you can't leave this patient here in the hospital for another day; you've got to get him out of here." I was not used to that. I had lived in the era when I was in charge.

I was also ready to give up my practice and leave California for Washington because I had my wife, Kathleen—known to her family and friends as "Kit"—to share the upheaval with me. Our youngest daughter, Kimberly, and several of her girlfriends had agreed to move into our house until we returned home. I felt I had all bases covered, including the fact that when I arrived in Washington I would be in the enviable position of not having to bow and scrape to keep my job, because I didn't need it. I was simply there for a short time to serve my country and my friend Ronald Reagan.

Journey to the White House

My journey to the White House began on November 20, 1980, a few days after Ronald Reagan had defeated Jimmy Carter in the battle for the presidency. I wrote a letter to President-elect Reagan's long-time lawyer and business adviser William French Smith, who had just been named attorney general in the upcoming Reagan Administration.

William French Smith and I belonged to the same country club, our wives had been high school classmates, his sister was a patient of mine, and I had been sending him my bills for treating Ronald Reagan months before he was elected governor of California in 1966. I told Smith I was sending a letter to Ronald Reagan suggesting that it would be a privilege for me, and helpful to him, if I became his White House physician. I also knew that his personal physician, Dr. John Sharpe, was in poor health, had retired from the practice of medicine, and might not be up to the task.

William French Smith mentioned this to the president-elect, who called me a few weeks later to say Mrs. Reagan's stepfather, Dr. Loyal Davis, a well-known Chicago neurosurgeon, had already made arrangements for his partner Dr. Daniel Ruge to be his White House doctor. Dr. Ruge had enjoyed an outstanding career as a professor of neurosurgery, was the author of two widely recognized textbooks on the subject (*Spinal Cord Injury* and *Spinal Cord Disability*), and had his name in *Who's Who in Medicine.* "One day," he told me, "I'm going to write a book called *Kitchens I've Eaten In* while waiting around for the president of the United States." Dr. Ruge is bound to go down in White House history for coining the phrase "The job is strictly blue collar."

I told Ronald Reagan I was sorry I couldn't be of service, and asked him if he could put me on the list for tickets to his inauguration on January 20, 1981, which he did. Kit and I flew to Washington for the inaugural on a special plane chartered by the southern California Republican delegation. The Reagan children were aboard, and it was party time until we touched down at Baltimore-Washington International Airport. We were all bused to the DuPont Plaza Hotel, which had taken on a convention atmosphere with signs, registration desks, and sign-up cards for various inauguration events.

The day before the inauguration was highlighted by Vice President Bush's reception, by the First Lady's luncheon and show, and finally by the glittering evening gala that continued into the wee hours. The next morning President-elect Reagan attended church, had lunch with President Jimmy Carter, and drove with him to the Capitol for the Inauguration Day swearing-in ceremony. Ronald Reagan broke with tradition by being sworn in on the Capitol's West Balcony, which provided him with a spectacular view of the Mall, the Washington Monument, the reflecting pool, the Lincoln Memorial, the Jefferson Memorial, and the White House, which would be his home for the next eight years.

The traditional inaugural parade began right after President Reagan's lunch with the Congress, moved down Pennsylvania Avenue, and ended at the White House. The president hardly had time to rest before he and Mrs. Reagan began making the rounds of all the white-tie dinner dances held in the capital's hotels and historical buildings. They made a grand entrance as the band played "Ruffles and Flourishes" and "Hail to the Chief." Guests roared their approval as the president and First Lady thanked them for their support, and then moved out onto the floor for the obligatory dance before moving on to the next celebration.

During the inaugural parade, and again during the gala dinner dance Kit and I attended, I realized that Ronald and Nancy Reagan were now living in another world. And that I would never again be as close to them as I had been in the past. Little did I know that in a few years, I would join them in that other world.

Kit and I spent a week in Washington during the inaugural celebrations, which gave me a chance to visit Dr. Ruge at the headquarters of the Veterans Administration, where he was director of the Spinal Cord Injury Service. I gave Dr. Ruge the president-elect's X rays and other medical records that I had on file at St. John's Hospital in Santa Monica, California, where I had treated him when he was governor of the state of California.

A little over a year later, toward the end of March 1982, Dr. Ruge called me in Los Angeles to say the president was having some urological symptoms, and asked if I could return to Washington for an April 1 consultation with Navy Captain Kevin O'Connell, M.D., chief of the Urology Department at the Naval Hospital in Bethesda, Maryland. I said I'd be delighted, and since I knew the president literally inside and out, I felt I might be useful. I had also planned to be in Washington anyway for a meeting of urologists, so the timing was perfect.

I flew into Washington on March 31, and that evening I went over to Dr. Ruge's office in the White House, where we sat around his television set and watched the president spar with reporters during a press conference. At about 9 P.M., we left his office and walked across the hall to the president's private elevator, which carried us up to the Reagans' private living quarters in the White House. The president and First Lady greeted me warmly, and introduced me to Chief of Staff James Baker, III, Counsel to the President Edwin Meese, and Deputy Chief of Staff Michael Deaver, whom I had known in California and who were all up there congratulating the president on the way he had just handled the press. The president said, "Gentlemen, you'll have to excuse me; my doctor's here," and as they marched off, the four of us began discussing the president's trip to Bethesda the following day. I listened to the president's description of his symptoms and agreed with Dr. Ruge that he should have a complete urological investigation.

Early the next morning, I was picked up by a White House car and driven to the Naval Hospital in Bethesda. As we turned off Wisconsin Avenue and into the hospital grounds, the driver pointed out the concrete pad surrounded by Navy security people where the president's helicopter was about to land.

I was taken to a small, secured entrance to the hospital, and was escorted to Captain Kevin O'Connell's medical office. Dr. O'Connell introduced me to his staff, and then we changed into surgical suits and left on a tour of the area where President Reagan would have his kidneys x-rayed and his urinary bladder and prostate examined with a cystoscope. A nearby room had been set aside for Mrs. Reagan and the president's staff.

As we walked back to Dr. O'Connell's office after the tour, I was amazed to see several uniformed men with K-9 dogs meticulously searching the area we had just left. They looked, and the dogs sniffed under chairs, behind pictures, and inside desks, lamps, and filing cabinets as they swept the room for bombs, hidden microphones, or anything else which might have been planted there to harm the president.

Secret Service agents patrolled the halls, and moments later the advance team arrived with word that President Reagan had left the White House and would arrive in less than ten minutes. The room's venetian blinds had been closed, but when I heard the president's helicopter overhead I separated the slats so I could watch him land. The police had stopped the heavy traffic on Wisconsin Avenue, and a fire truck and ambulance had moved into position beside the landing pad, now surrounded by plainclothesmen and Navy security personnel.

The president's olive-green helicopter, with its white top and the words United States of America and the presidential seal painted on its side, gently touched down on the landing pad's colored marker disks. The huge rotors slowed to a halt, and the front and rear doors were lowered, forming metal stairs to the ground as Secret Service agents and armed Marines surrounded the helicopter and the president's motorcade moved into position. President Reagan was alone (the First Lady had a prior speaking engagement), and as he exited from the front of the helicopter the staff, including Dr. Ruge carrying his tan medical bag, left from the rear. The president climbed into his armored limousine, and the motorcade took off on its seven-second drive to the hospital's entrance, where reporters and photographers stood ready to record his arrival. President Reagan could have strolled to the hospital in no time. But the Secret Service insisted on the motorcade.

Dr. O'Connell and I were waiting in his medical office when the door was flung open and President Reagan and his entourage poured in. Quick introductions were made, White House staff people were shown to their waiting room, and we prepared to examine the president, who was changing from his street clothes into a green hospital gown. I was amazed by the efficiency of it all. Everyone knew exactly what to do in order not to break the most cardinal of all White House rules, i.e., "You don't keep the president of the United States waiting."

President Reagan was given a local anesthetic which would eliminate discomfort, but would not impair his ability to run the country as its chief executive. This meant we did not have to transfer his powers to Vice President Bush under the Twenty-fifth Amendment to the Constitution. The examination indicated that the president had a moderately enlarged prostate gland, but since this was quite acceptable for a man his age we felt no further treatment was called for at this time. I must say we were all relieved that everything had turned out so well.

The president's deputy chief of staff, Mike Deaver, suggested we work up a statement for the press on the results of Mr. Reagan's examination. Larry Speakes, the president's press spokesman, manned the typewriter, and they both turned to me to tell them what to say. I told them a complete urological examination had been performed that included a "physical examination, an X ray of the kidneys made by injecting dye, and a look into his urinary bladder and prostate. He has an enlarged prostate in keeping with his age. No cancer was found and no further treatment is necessary at this time." This was my first involvement with a White House press release, but as I was to learn to my sorrow, it would not be my last.

The president dressed, and he and his staff left as quickly as they had arrived. I walked out with Mr. Reagan, who was instantly greeted by a barrage of questions from the waiting press: "Are you all right?" "Did it hurt?" The questions kept coming, but were drowned out by the racket from the helicopter's rotor blades. The president invited me to return with him to the White House, but before answering I glanced at Dr. Ruge, who nodded his agreement, so I joined him in the motorcade for the dash to the helicopter.

The Sikorsky helicopter's interior was upholstered with presidential blue material, could seat ten people, and was officially known as Marine Helicopter Squadron One, or HMX1. The president sat facing forward on the left beside a large picture window so he could see, be seen, and wave to the crowd. The First Lady's seat was directly across from the president's and faced aft with a small folding table between them. The staff sat on a bench seat on the right side of the helicopter. Dr. Ruge sat forward opposite the president followed by the military aide, Deputy Chief of Staff Mike Deaver, Larry Speakes, a Secret Service agent and myself. When everyone was strapped in and settled, the military aide gave the sign and the doors were slammed shut and secured. What a day this had been, and now here I was riding in the White House helicopter with the president of the United States and surrounded by the president's men—unreal!

The helicopter's huge rotor blades began to turn, and then gathered speed as the Secret Service agent sitting next to me said into his microphone, "We have a departure. We have a departure." These words would be relayed to many stations along our route as they followed the president's flight, and I would hear them hundreds of times in the years ahead. We were now comfortably airborne, and the view down below was dramatic as we circled the Naval Hospital in Bethesda and headed southeast to the White House. The president motioned for me to come forward and sit opposite him in the First Lady's seat so he could show me points of interest as we flew along. What a way to see Washington, with the most important person in the world as my guide!

We flew down the Potomac River and then turned east to the Mall for our approach to the White House grounds. President Reagan pointed out the huge Central Intelligence Agency complex, Georgetown University, the Watergate apartments, Kennedy Center, Arlington National Cemetery, the Lincoln and Jefferson memorials, the towering Washington Monument, and the Tidal Basin with its hundreds of cherry trees in full bloom. The president instructed his military aide to tell the pilot to circle the Tidal Basin once more for a better look at the cherry blossoms, which were a spectacular sight when seen from the air on this crystal clear day.

We were now approaching the White House, flying just above the South Lawn with its fountain, trees, tennis court, and pool off to the left. The helicopter touched down so its doors would open toward the

White House for additional security. President Reagan emerged, gave his familiar thumbs up sign to the crowd, and headed toward a battery of cameras, microphones, and reporters yelling questions at him. He said, "Everything is fine, and now I have to get back to the Oval Office, roll up my sleeves, and get back to work." The president went upstairs to change into a business suit, while I joined Dr. Ruge in his office, never dreaming that in the very near future I would be there.

I was driven back to my hotel in a White House car, but asked the driver to stop by a men's clothing store so I could buy a blue shirt. I was convinced, in my innocence, that television stations would be hounding me for an interview about the morning I had just spent with the president and understood that a blue shirt was the thing to wear. My phone never did ring, even though the six o'clock news carried a story about the president's trip to the hospital and his arrival back at the White House. I did spot myself for a second or two standing under the helicopter on the White House lawn with my hair being blown all over the place.

Dr. Ruge continued to look after Ronald Reagan as his White House physician, but when the president decided to run for a second term in 1984 Dr. Ruge called me to see if I'd be interested in being his replacement. I told him I would, and in July 1984, my wife, Kit, and I returned to Washington.

Dr. Ruge had arranged for us to see the president in the Oval Office the next day. He escorted us there, and then left us alone with the president, who was warm and gracious, and led us over to two sofas and twin straight-backed chairs. The president told Kit to sit in his chair, and asked me to take the vice president's chair while he sat on one of the sofas. I led off the conversation by telling the president I'd be pleased to supervise his medical affairs; he then showed us several items in the Oval Office, and we left feeling everything had gone quite well.

We had a delightful dinner that evening with Dr. Ruge and his wife at their home. As we were chatting, Dr. Ruge suddenly left the room to take a call from President Reagan on the direct line he had to the White House. When he returned, Dr. Ruge said the president had told him he would be happy to have me as his personal physician if he were reelected. I was now committed. There would be no turning back. And I was about to experience the two most extraordinary years in my life, filled with nonstop excitement.

Kit and I returned home to Los Angeles, and the next thing I knew *Parade* magazine's Lloyd Shearer had written in his "Intelligence

Report" column for August 12, 1984, that Dr. T. Burton Smith, a "handsome, personable, tennis-playing M.D. who's cared for many a Hollywood star," was being groomed to replace Dr. Daniel Ruge as President Reagan's personal physician. I was astonished since only a handful of people, accustomed to keeping secrets, knew of my coming move to Washington. It was my first experience with a "leak," but by no means my last.

By this time I felt I should discuss the possibility of becoming the president's doctor with my family, and received distinctly mixed signals. My ninety-six-year-old mother said, "Go for it." My wife said, "Do whatever you want." And my three daughters and son said, "Ah come on, Dad, you've worked hard all your life, and you're just starting to play golf and have fun. Why in the world do you want to get back into harness again?"

In November, Kit and I left for China with the People-to-People Tennis program started by President Dwight Eisenhower. I served as team physician. While we were gone, President Reagan was running for a second term against Walter Mondale, and we weren't able to find out who had won until we flew out of China, landed in Hong Kong, and turned on the television in our room in the Mandarin Hotel. The moment I learned the president had won by a landslide—taking all but one of the fifty states—I rushed downstairs to the hotel's tailor shop, run by a Mr. Chen, and said, "Quick, make me a couple of dark suits so I will look 'presidential'!" I also realized I had nothing "presidential" to wear in the event of an emergency if I had to rush to Ronald Reagan's side in the middle of the night. So I ordered contrasting white and brown monogrammed pajamas with matching bathrobe which I faithfully took with me everywhere we went but fortunately never had to use.

We flew to Washington on November 24, 1985, and began searching for a place to live. We eventually chose the Watergate South Apartments because if an emergency arose, I could jump in a White House car with siren screaming and be by the president's side in under five minutes. The FBI also told me the Watergate was reasonably secure despite its notoriety. This was important since, among other things, I planned to walk the half dozen blocks or so to work and back whenever possible.

My appointment as the president's doctor had not been officially announced when on November 26, *Time* magazine columnist Hugh Sidey wrote that Dr. Ruge "has been training a replacement, Los Angeles physician Burton Smith, for more than a year." I don't know where he got his information, but I was to get more deeply involved with leaks to the press before my tour of duty with the president was over.

I was officially named White House doctor a few weeks later, and given an impressive looking certificate embossed with the Great Seal of the United States and signed by Secretary of State George Shultz who was the keeper of the Great Seal embossing machine which retracted each night into a vault in the State Department. I was now a bona fide member of President Reagan's White House staff, although this would later change when my slot was needed for a political operative, and my pay-card was transferred to the Defense Department.

Kit and I were busily tagging furniture for the big move when we were told that Uncle Sam did not pay to bring the president's new doctor to Washington. Then I received a bunch of questionnaires to complete for my FBI clearance demanding information going clear back to my high school days. They covered my years in the service during World War II when we made thirteen moves (they wanted to know the date of each move plus the street number of every house we had lived in). I was also asked to provide details on the dozens of trips Kit and I had taken outside the U.S., facts on our family finances, and other personal information which tempted me to quit then and there because I hate filling out forms. The deputy counsel to the president, H. Lawrence Garrett, III, came to my rescue when he called and said, "Sit down, Doctor, and we'll complete those forms together." Had it not been for this patient man, I'm sure I would have returned home. Garrett was secretary of the Navy until his recent resignation.

So Kit and I persevered, and began preparing for the move. We slashed the things we wanted to take with us to a handful of items such as our garden furniture which we planned to use in the living room, and figured we'd buy a bed, a television set and so on when we arrived in Washington. Yet we still ended up spending $3,000 on the move, and at least $3,000 on the move back home again to Los Angeles.

We had our fully loaded Buick station wagon driven to Washington, D.C., by a college student from George Washington University who was visiting California. We had considered taking a foreign-made car we also owned, but decided it wouldn't be right putting a foreign car in the White House executive parking lot. Since I was going to be an employee of the United States government as of January 1, 1985, I thought I should use products "Made in the U.S.A." But when I drove my Buick into the White House parking lot for the first time, I discovered it was filled with every foreign car in the book.

On December 31, 1984, Kit and I were driven to the Los Angeles airport and took our seats in the economy section of the late-night "red eye special," since presidential appointees are not paid for travel. We had brought along a bottle of champagne to celebrate the New Year and our new life in the nation's capital, but were so tired we immediately fell asleep. When we awoke it was 1985 and we were coming into Washington. Our great adventure was about to begin.

Chapter Two

"Celebrity Doctor" Comes to Washington

Larry Speakes, the president's press spokesman, called me a "semi-retired celebrity doctor" in his book *Speaking Out,* which I guess I was since my medical practice in Los Angeles included well-known people such as band leader Lawrence Welk and movie star Cornel Wilde, along with prominent sports personalities and, of course, Governor Ronald Reagan.

A few members of the White House medical staff felt I wasn't a "whole doctor" since I was a urological surgeon specializing in the urogenital tract. But it was a urologist Ronald Reagan needed on March 14, 1966—two months before he entered politics as a candidate for governor of California—when his family physician, Dr. John Sharpe, called me to the Reagan home on San Onofre Drive in Pacific Palisades to treat him for a lower urinary tract infection.

Ronald Reagan was obviously ill with a recurrent fever, yet he kept doggedly campaigning against California's Democratic incumbent Governor Edmund "Pat" Brown. I couldn't understand it. Here he was a noted actor, a family man with children, financially well-off, had been head of the Screen Actors Guild, was working as a highly paid spokesman for General Electric, and at fifty-five was no kid anymore. I remember saying to him, during one of his visits to my office, "You know every time you stress yourself in this campaign you run a fever, and symptoms associated with your urinary tract infection recur. Why do you insist on doing this to yourself?"

"Two reasons," he said. "I think the people of California deserve a better governor than Pat Brown. And secondly it kind of gets to you when you go to one of these political rallies. You drive up, there's all the commotion, people shaking your hand. Then they throw open the doors and the band's playing, the lights are on, the balloons are cascading down, the flags are waving, and everybody's shouting. It kind of gets you in here," he said, stabbing a finger into his chest. I didn't appreciate what he was saying then, but I do now having accompanied him to numerous political rallies and getting chills every time I did. It's like the kickoff at a football game; the anticipation and excitement move you like few things can.

On January 5, 1967, Kit and I were invited up to Sacramento, California, to help celebrate Ronald Reagan's inauguration as governor after he defeated Pat Brown by nearly a million votes. There was a big preinauguration reception, and his $1,000 supporters were wined, dined, and had their pictures taken shaking hands with the new governor. We bypassed this because we couldn't afford it and besides, I could shake hands with him anytime I wanted to. But as I was to learn later, people would line up to have their picture taken with Ronald Reagan, and after he became president they happily paid a lot more than $1,000 for this brief photo opportunity.

I was called in that summer to examine Ronald Reagan, who was again having urinary tract problems, and immediately discovered that the governor of California had no designated doctor. So on July 28, 1967, I admitted him to Saint John's Hospital, where he was visited by Mrs. Reagan's stepfather, Dr. Loyal Davis. I had talked to Dr. Davis a year or so earlier when he called to ask me how to treat Ronald Reagan for a urinary tract infection which developed when he and Nancy were staying with him in Chicago.

I operated on Governor Reagan on July 31 to relieve his suffering from an infected and stone-ridden prostate gland. I did a transurethral resection of the bladder neck, removing some of the prostate gland, which proved to be noncancerous, along with about thirty bladder stones. I discharged him from the hospital on August 5, 1968, to be followed by a three-week recovery period. I've often wondered if I hadn't done that operation, and if it hadn't turned out as well as it did, Ronald Reagan might not have ended up as our fortieth president.

Trouble with the *New York Times*

It was during this operation on Governor Reagan that I had the first of several annoying experiences with the media. The first occurred after the 1968 operation when a paper ran a headline saying something like "Governor Ronald Reagan's West Coast Doctor Removes His Gallstones Through Normal Channels Using a Telescope." This was dead wrong. Bladder stones were removed through the normal urinary channel in those days—not gallstones. This headline made me a laughingstock among my fellow urologists. So much so that when I attended the regular yearly meeting of the British Association of Urological Surgeons in London, they got everybody in a relaxed mood by throwing the headline up on the screen instead of the usual nude photo or cartoon. And they did it not knowing I was in the audience.

My first run-in with the *New York Times* was in 1981, not long after Governor Reagan had been nominated for president. The paper sent its medical correspondent, Lawrence K. Altman, M.D., to Los Angeles to interview me and the Reagans' family physician, John Reynolds, on the state of Mr. Reagan's health. Altman had decided Ronald Reagan was senile, and he tried to get us to agree with him, which was nonsense. Altman struck again in March 1982, when I was asked to return to Washington to oversee an examination of the president's urinary system, which ended in my giving him a clean bill of health. This time Altman's paper wrote that we had injected radioactive substances into the president when we x-rayed his kidneys which was, again, totally wrong. The antiradiation group was incensed.

I continued to see Ronald Reagan professionally from time to time until I became his White House physician. I had quit my medical practice cold two months before leaving for Washington, and had gone back to work at Saint John's Hospital in order to get more of the kind of experience I might need in looking after the president of the United States. I worked in the hospital's cardiac care unit, intensive care unit, and recovery room. I hooked up heart patients to electrocardiogram machines, and then read the result. I inserted intravenous drips into the veins of a lot of patients so I'd be proficient even in the middle of the night, or out on the street. I answered all the hospital emergency codes calling for doctors to rush to the side of patients having heart attacks. I did all this for about six weeks, trying to become more of a whole doctor and not just a urologist.

When I finally left for Washington I felt confident I could handle any medical emergency involving the president. But the doctors and nurses who were already working in the White House weren't so sure about me, their new boss. So to be on the safe side, and help put their minds at ease, I went on to complete two 3-day intensive courses at a Washington military hospital in acute coronary life support and acute trauma life support. It was seventy-two hours of nonstop reading, instruction, and drilling. I'd pretend, for example, that I was the head of a team which comes upon somebody twenty-eight years old who's been in a motorcycle accident. He smells of alcohol, can't breathe, and needs immediate care. So boom, I'd start giving everybody orders. You do this, you do that, until the patient is out of danger and stabilized.

I was in the habit of taking thorough annual physical examinations, but when I became President Reagan's doctor I stepped them up considerably by adding things like stress tests to find out if I was at any risk from a heart attack. I certainly didn't want to get hit with a heart attack while flying over the Pacific Ocean in Air Force One so that instead of me looking after the president, he'd have to worry about who was looking after me. The answer to that question is nobody. I was the only medically trained person among the fifty or so people aboard Air Force One, and although I had given the eight or ten Secret Service agents on the plane a course in CPR (cardiopulmonary resuscitation), there's a lot of difference between learning and doing.

An Honorary License to Practice Medicine

Many doctors believe presidential physicians should have their medical competence certified by a peer review panel, and then have their appointment confirmed by the Senate just like nominees to the Supreme Court. The president, however, can choose any doctor he wants, or any other member of his personal staff for that matter.

I didn't even have to be licensed to practice medicine in Washington, D.C., because the White House is considered to be a self-governing island within the district, not unlike a foreign embassy. The District of Columbia Medical Society did give me an honorary license to practice in the capital which I thought was a nice gesture, and it accepted my national narcotics license.

I was aware of the tension between the president and Congress as to exactly what constitutes medical competence. The Army and Navy doctors on my White House staff had to pass a yearly military physical exam, as well as a qualification report done by their immediate superior (rather like the one I did for my chief assistant, Dr. John Hutton, who was on assignment to the White House from the U.S. Army). But no one ever did a physical or competence report on me. The president wanted me for his doctor and that was that. Now if I had been always late getting to work, if I had always seemed inattentive, or if I had always had a martini in my hand, someone might have blown the whistle. But it would take this kind of unorthodox behavior before the president would be advised that he had made a poor choice of doctors and should get somebody else.

Washington journalists seem to delight in pointing out just how low the president's physician is on the White House totem pole; it's something like number fifty-four on a list of fifty-five. My office in the White House basement seemed to bear this out, since it was near the office of the cook, the housekeeper, and the flower arranger. So did the fact that when I'd accompany the president to parties, like the one he attended at the home of Secretary of State George Shultz, I'd be stationed in the garage or some other holding room for hours until it was time to return to the White House.

This didn't bother me, and I accepted it cheerfully since it comes with the territory. I was not part of the Washington power structure; I was Ronald Reagan's doctor. My job was to look after the health of the president of the United States. But if access to the president is the ultimate card anyone can hold in Washington—and it is—my hand was unbeatable. I was one of perhaps a half-dozen people who could enter the president's Oval Office unannounced. I was often with him for days on end, and alone with him for hours at a time. Yet I never mentioned anything to do with politics or affairs of state, which is probably the reason we got along so well.

The president and I had known each other for eighteen years when I became his White House doctor. We were contemporaries (when I arrived in Washington he was seventy-three and I was sixty-eight, making us perhaps the oldest doctor-president team in U.S. history). We were dyed-in-the wool southern Californians who had both worked in the movie industry; he as an actor, and I as a new doctor who occasionally picked up $25 a day going out on location with MGM crews shooting films with Alan Ladd and other stars in which dangerous stunts were to be performed. Twenty-five bucks was a small fortune to me back then, since I was making only $10 a month plus room and board as a young intern slaving away in a county hospital.

My Topflight Medical Team

Once the president chooses you as his personal physician, your next job is to put together a topflight medical team from among military doctors and nurses recommended by the armed forces. Mine consisted of fourteen people including four doctors: Colonel John Hutton, a general surgeon in the U.S. Army, who had been brought in by my predecessor, Dr. Ruge; Navy Lieutenant Commanders Kenneth Lee and Rodney Savage; and Air Force Major Robert Gasser, all of whom were internists. I had Dr. Hutton look after President Reagan in my absence, and I assigned Drs. Lee, Savage, and Gasser to keep an eye on Vice President Bush. While we each had our individual responsibilities, we worked closely together as a team. Dr. Savage, for example, is a fine cardiologist, and I'd always ask him to evaluate President Reagan's heart whenever I gave the president a physical examination.

I made Dr. Hutton my chief of staff because he's a good general and vascular surgeon and familiar to the president. Dr. Hutton had been chief of surgery at the Letterman Army Hospital in San Francisco, and at the Walter Reed Army Medical Center in Washington, D.C. He had also served as a surgeon in the Korean and Vietnam wars, and had done research on ballistics and trauma.

One of Dr. Hutton's greatest attributes was that he knew how to get things done through the military. When we needed doctors to work in the White House he'd ask the Army, Navy, and Air Force to send us the profiles of those they thought could do the job, even if they were on duty in Spain or somewhere else thousands of miles from Washington. We'd cull them over and select the ones we wanted to call in for interviews knowing that their superiors would never refuse our request since we were acting for their commander in chief.

Alone with the President

Two people accompanied President Reagan everywhere he went. I was one, and the other was the military aide who carried a slim briefcase—known as the "football"—containing the secret military communications codes the president would use to order a retaliatory strike against the then Soviet Union or any other country which attacked the United States with nuclear weapons. Officers from the Air Force, Army, Coast Guard, Navy, and Marines would take turns carrying the "football" for anywhere from several hours to a week when on duty at the isolated Reagan ranch near Santa Barbara, California. They're also responsible for handling all communications between the military and the president, and deciding in advance where to rush the president if his life is in danger, no matter where he happens to be anywhere in the world. Carrying the "football" is their prime responsibility, yet on one occasion an officer walked off without it and had to backtrack in double time to retrieve it.

I was the only staff person who was allowed to be alone with the president even though my tan medical bag contained several potentially lethal drugs and the needles to inject them. Beyond that, nobody was quite sure what I was doing or what kinds of potions I was mixing up. But even when I was alone with the president he was surrounded by security. There was a "panic button" next to his bed in the White House in case he needed to summon help. And there was always an armed Secret Service man right outside the door of his White House living quarters, the presidential retreat at Camp David, the Reagan ranch, the Bethesda Naval Medical Center, or wherever he happened to be. Don Regan said he was never alone with the president for a single minute during the time he was secretary of the treasury and a member of the president's cabinet. This changed, however, after he swapped jobs with James Baker, became President Reagan's chief of staff, and was assigned a Secret Service agent to protect his life.

I was also the only person who could give the president of the United States a direct order and expect him to obey it, which he always did with good humor. Soon after his surgery for colon cancer in July 1985, for example, he strode into his private pool at Camp David and started swimming like he must have done when he was a lifeguard in his youth. He'd gone only a few yards when I told him to dog paddle around until the incision in his abdomen became stronger.

If the president, his driver, and the Secret Service agents accompanying him were all shot by a gunman, or injured in an automobile accident, I would order that the president be treated first. But, knowing him, he'd probably tell me to look after the others first. This, however, was my decision—not his. He could order me to "Take care of Agent Jones first because he has a wife and three small children." And I'd still have to say, "Sorry, Mr. President, I'm going to look after you first, and then I'll get to Agent Jones and the others." One reason, in addition to the fact that he's the president, is that he might have no idea just how badly hurt he really is, which was the case after he was shot by John Hinkley, Jr. He might have a potentially fatal ruptured spleen and not even know it, or he might have injured his brain, which is not so bad at the outset but all of a sudden—bang—you're dead.

Change of Direction

As you probably realize by now, and certainly will by the time you finish this book, I was never more than a few minutes away from the president's side twenty-four hours a day. This is where I was told to be, and this is where I wanted to be, since the first few minutes following a medical emergency can determine whether the president will live or die.

This doctor-president relationship is not carved in stone, and President Bush's White House physician, Dr. Burton J. Lee, III, has changed it. Dr. Lee, who was a member of President Reagan's AIDS Commission, is a cancer specialist who practiced at the highly regarded Memorial Sloan-Kettering Cancer Center in New York, and has been George Bush's friend for many years. Dr. Lee calls the president "George," whereas I always addressed Ronald Reagan as "Mr. President." I was equally formal with George Bush when we worked together, always calling him "Mr. Vice President." Maybe it's because I'm a little older, a little more conventional.

Dr. Lee and I, as mentioned earlier, also differ on how close the doctor should be to his patient. I was near President Reagan all the time, whereas Dr. Lee has outside professional interests which take him away from the White House from time to time, and which President Bush knew about before asking him to serve as his White House doctor.

On these occasions, Dr. Lee will ask another doctor on his staff to look after President Bush, who is tremendously active and a challenge to any doctor assigned to keep up with him. So much so that following the president's annual medical checkup on March 26, 1992—less than three weeks before his sixty-ninth birthday—Dr. Lee told the press that although Mr. Bush was in robust good health, he thought he needed to cut back his hectic schedule and take vacations more often.

I'm very sympathetic with Dr. Lee's suggestion because the doctors I assigned to look after Mr. Bush when he was vice president were led on a merry chase because he was always on the go, much like Vice President Dan Quayle is today. It was always "You die, I fly" when he had to represent President Reagan at the funeral of a foreign statesman. Yet I never heard George Bush complain. His only gripe was that he was surrounded by too many Secret Service agents (it was two or three back then, and now that he's president it's probably two or three dozen).

Dr. Lee and I also see things differently when it comes to expanding the White House doctor's job to include advising the president on medical policy issues. He wants to do it, and I think the idea has merit. But President Reagan never expressed any desire to discuss medical policies with me, and I never advocated any to him.

Dr. Lee plans to rely heavily on Barbara Bush if the president becomes disabled and those around him begin considering temporarily transferring his power to Vice President Quayle under the Twenty-fifth Amendment to the Constitution. Dr. Lee says Mrs. Bush is "a level-headed woman with such good judgment that she would be a terrific ally" in deciding whether or not the president is capable of carrying out his duties. Dr. Lee has said he could not conceive of President Bush ever becoming depressed, emotionally unstable, or unable to carry out his duties, but that "the trickiest part" of his job would be in dealing with such problems should they ever arise. Dr. Lee quickly adds that he has no intention of ever adding a psychiatrist to his White House medical staff.

While I assigned two of my junior physicians to look after George Bush, there were times when I thought how enjoyable it would be to take this duty myself, since he and I both love tennis. I'm also delighted to report, in view of the concern about his dying prematurely, that George Bush is a very vital, very healthy man. His recent checkups have been good, he's in really great physical shape, and he has a very positive attitude toward life.

If George Bush has a physical problem, at least in the minds of the Secret Service agents, military aide, and medical people who accompany him everywhere he goes, it's probably his passion for roaring around in his speedboat when he's up at his place in Kennebunkport, Maine. They are in the speedboat with him when he tools the thing up and takes off through the water, knocking them all over the place. He's driving, so he can anticipate the bangs and crashes, but they can't. The Secret Service has a chase boat that follows along in case there's an accident or attack, and these agents too get beaten up. They don't like that. In fact, the two young doctors I assigned to Mr. Bush when he was vice president used to come back from these outings pretty well bruised up, and needing a little time off for rest and recuperation.

Unexpected Benefits

I enjoyed quite a few perquisites as a member of President Reagan's senior staff. I always had a dark blue White House Chrysler LeBaron car and driver at my beck and call but preferred to walk when I could. While most of the staff riding with the president aboard Air Force One exited from the rear, I left from the front so I'd be there in case he fell or stumbled down the steps.

I could get all the free aspirin and pills I wanted from the White House pharmacy, although this didn't amount to much since Kit and I are not great medicine takers. I could have my shoes shined during my daily 11 A.M. workouts at the White House gym. And I could play tennis on the White House court with other staffers such as Mike Deaver, who moved like greased lightning—not on the court, but in the locker room. Mike would be showered, dressed, and out of there after a match before I'd even unlaced my tennis shoes.

I never saw the president use the White House tennis court, although members of his cabinet did. My wife and I were playing one Sunday morning when Secretary of State George Shultz and *Washington Post* owner Katharine Graham showed up in separate limousines, and I figured it was time for us to leave the court. Mrs. Shultz doesn't play tennis because of a game leg, and was known to go after her husband to help improve his communication skills.

Everyone on the White House senior staff got a daily news summary prepared by the president's Office of the Press Secretary, and at the end of the week we got the "Friday Follies," filled with press cartoons about the Reagans and other members of the administration. One of the funniest cartoons was always reproduced on the cover, right above a comment made by New York political boss William Marcy Tweed in 1871 to Thomas Nast, the famed cartoonist for *Harper's Weekly:* "I don't care a straw for your newspaper articles," said Boss Tweed. "My constituents don't know how to read. But they can't help seeing those damned pictures."

The president liked the "Friday Follies" more than did the First Lady, who was terribly incensed by one cartoon which appeared after a mentally disturbed, but unarmed man named Robert Latta slipped past the security guards and marched into the White House behind the Marine Band, which was getting ready to play at President Reagan's second Inauguration Day swearing-in ceremony. He was later found wandering around below the Reagans' living quarters, and the cartoon showed him snuggled up between the president and First Lady in their White House bed. The next day, as the president was walking from the White House to the Old Executive Office Building to address a group of businesspeople, he turned to his Secret Service escort and said, "Have you taken a count to make sure there aren't any strangers among us?"

One of the hallways in the West Wing of the White House was always decorated with jumbo-size color photographs of the president and First Lady taken by several White House staff photographers who recorded their every move for posterity. If you liked one of the jumbos you could write your name on the back, and when it was taken down you could have it so long as no one higher up on the totem pole wanted it as well. While I was near the bottom of this pecking order, I did manage to get half a dozen or so terrific jumbos showing everything from the president giving a press conference (a great shot looking into the taut faces of a hundred or more reporters and photographers trying to get his attention) to a lovely one of a smiling First Lady hugging the president around the waist (which makes me wince every time I see it because the president's abdomen had not completely healed following his July 1985 operation for colon cancer).

One of my favorite jumbos is of President and Mrs. Reagan standing on the bridge of the USS *Iowa* celebrating the one hundredth birthday of the Statue of Liberty in New York Harbor on July 4, 1986. It's a terrific jumbo, now on display in the hall outside my study at home, showing the Air Force Thunderbirds flying by overhead, trailing streams of red, white and blue smoke, and hundreds of ships bobbing about in the water below. The white "toe marks" indicating exactly where Ronald and Nancy Reagan should stand on the battleship's bridge are clearly visible, which is a major no-no and was undoubtedly brought to the attention of the aide responsible for the oversight. I understand that Carter Administration jumbos were removed from the halls of the White House within minutes after Ronald Reagan became president, and that Reagan-era jumbos vanished just as quickly after George Bush moved into the Oval Office.

Basking in the President's Shadow

Our apartment in the Watergate was right opposite the Kennedy Center for the Performing Arts. President Reagan had a private box in each of the center's three theaters which he'd use on occasions such as when his friend Charlton Heston was starring as Captain Queeg in *The Caine Mutiny Court-Martial.* If the president or First Lady was not using their box, they would generously offer it to White House staff members. From time to time my wife, Kit, and I would have the box to ourselves and were able to see the Broadway hit *Les Misérables*, conductor and cellist Mstislav Rostropovich, and other superb performances from the greatest seats in the house. The presidential box seated twelve, which meant we were able to entertain family and friends in style. The box was roped off, had a private bathroom, and a

closet filled with soft drinks and splits of champagne bearing the
presidential seal. There was a telephone in the box with a red call light
which the White House could use if the president needed me, even
though I never went anywhere without a paging beeper attached to
my belt.

The White House advance office always seemed to have extra staff
tickets for theatrical events attended by the president, and I'd often
get some so I could take Kit and occasionally a friend visiting us from
out of town. I did this once after leaving the White House when the
president was speaking at a World Affairs Council luncheon in Los
Angeles. The advance office was happy to give me two extra $500 staff
tickets which allowed me to sit with my old buddies and say hello to
former Senator Howard Baker, who had just replaced Don Regan as
the president's chief of staff.

Since I accompanied President Reagan everywhere he went, I was
able to sample some of the greatest cuisine in the world, although
always at a table set aside for the staff. The president belonged to
Washington's illustrious Alfalfa Club, whose one hundred or so members and their guests got together once a year for a fabulous dinner
and memorable liquid refreshment. I asked the president why it was
called the Alfalfa Club, and he said, "It was named for the alfalfa plant,
which has a long tap root that will go anywhere to find a drink."

I was a member of the president's party at these affairs, which
meant my dinner was on the house. This was not the case, however,
when I ate in the White House dining room, at Camp David, aboard
Air Force One, at the Reagan ranch, or while on duty with the
president at some overseas billet such as the Aga Khan's mansion,
which we used during a conference in Geneva, Switzerland. While I
received a food allowance of $30 a day when we were on the road,
anything above that came out of my pocket. Once when I was staying
with President Reagan on the top floor of a Tokyo hotel and was about
to accompany him to an official black-tie dinner party that I knew
would run late, I stopped by the kitchen that was part of the presidential suite and had a cup of coffee. Two months later I received a bill for
fifty cents, which I promptly paid.

A week rarely went by when Kit and I didn't receive invitations to
parties and receptions, although we quickly learned that in Washington, D.C., positions—not people—get invited out. I was much higher
up in ceremonial rank than I was in political rank, and as a result
carried on an active social life. There's a saying in Washington that
"It's not who you are, but what you are that gets the invitations."

Chapter Three

My Early Life in Medicine

I knew one thing for sure as I was growing up—I was not going to be a medical doctor. My father was a doctor and I had watched him work brutally long days, come home with the smell of ether still on his clothes after a late afternoon surgery, miss dinner with the family, and eat alone with the telephone constantly ringing, or be awakened before dawn by a frantic mother begging him to come and look at her sick child. This was no life for me. I wanted to be a sportswriter like Lee Tracy in the movies with his press card, reporter's notebook, and easy access to places where hard-charging athletes were getting their names in the record books.

Father's family, like many others in the 1800s, had migrated westward to the good life they believed awaited them in America's heartland. My great grandfather had been drawn there after earning a medical degree, and had settled his family in Fulton, Missouri. Doctoring was a hard life back then, but he somehow found time to become town mayor, put in streets and a sewer system, and even run the local mental asylum.

My great grandfather's children continued our family's trek west with my grandfather settling in Gainesville, Texas, where he went into banking. Grandfather had five sons: three of them shared his love of business, and my father and his younger brother followed their grandfather into medicine.

Father was sent to the Morgan Park Academy in Chicago, which prepared students for the University of Chicago. Father made the academy's football and baseball teams, and he must have been talented because when he moved on to the university he pitched for its baseball team, and played football for the legendary coach Amos Alanzo Stagg. My father's name was Turner Burton Smith, which his baseball buddies abbreviated to "TB," pronounced "Tibby." His name lives on with my son Turner Burton Smith, III.

Father received his Doctor of Medicine degree from the University of Chicago's Rush Medical School in 1906, and decided to do his internship and surgical residency at Presbyterian Hospital rather than the sprawling Cook County General Hospital. Few doctors specialized in those days, but Father was intrigued by the factories in and around Chicago and decided to become an industrial surgeon.

One of Father's first positions was with the Phelps Dodge Copper Company's mining operation in the isolated little mining town of Morenci, Arizona. The rapid industrialization of the American economy had created a booming demand for copper, and Father jumped at the chance to be head surgeon at several community hospitals with enough time left over to hunt, fish, golf, and play tennis. He liked the place so well that he convinced several of his medical school classmates to join him, and even began thinking about how nice it would be if he were married.

The young lady my father would eventually marry came from a family whose roots were in Virginia, but eventually migrated to Springfield, Missouri, where her father sold farm tools. In the early 1900s, my mother's family of three girls and two boys moved to Los Angeles, California, where her father again sold farm implements (apparently quite successfully as they lived near the present University of Southern California campus). Mother commuted by streetcar to Los Angeles High School, graduated in 1906, and went on to a normal school to prepare for a career in teaching.

Somewhere along the line fate intervened and my father's mother, with five sons, met my mother's mother, with three girls and two boys. The women decided my father should meet the oldest of the three girls, so it was arranged that he travel to California and take her on a steamer day trip to Catalina Island. She accepted, provided her youngest sister could tag along. The predictable happened, of course, and my father fell in love with the younger sister. After many impassioned letters, and several trips back to California, he was able to convince her that marriage to an older doctor working in a faraway mining town was a rather romantic idea and so the knot was tied. Since the trip to Catalina Island had proved so rewarding, my father decided to take his bride on a five-day steamer cruise to faraway Hawaii, spending their honeymoon at the Moana Hotel on a desolate stretch of the island known as Waikiki Beach.

Life in a western mining town soon after the turn of the century was a rough experience for my mother, who was a city girl born and bred. There were few conveniences, and what social life she had was confined to occasional get-togethers with families of Phelps Dodge managers and engineers. My father was always busy with his medical work, but the two of them did get away from time to time to visit friends on the West Coast, or travel to Chicago for meetings of the American College of Surgeons.

I have vivid memories of Morenci, which was shaped like one of the craters of the moon. The Phelps Dodge offices, company store, school, and town plaza were on the bottom, with homes and copper mining operations climbing up the sides. We had a large company house next to the hospital and clinic, and when my father wasn't working there he'd be making house calls on horseback or on foot.

I was fascinated by the immensity of the copper operations, particularly the huge trucks which carried the ore from the mine to the rail terminal after it had been crushed and separated leaving a white residue that was fed into ponds which went on for miles. The stuff eventually evaporated creating large, flat, dry lakes which some Scotsmen among the mine's managers decided should be turned into a golf course. So they put oil on the sand to create the "greens," painted their golf balls orange, and teed off. My father learned to play golf on this course and immediately became hooked. He played the game religiously and well until a few years before his death at age ninety-five.

My mother became pregnant in Morenci, but traveled to California to give birth to us. Children born to Caucasians in Arizona back in those days rarely survived the summer because of the heat and poor sanitation. They contracted something called the "summer complaint" or "summer sickness" and died of terminal diarrhea. So my mother would leave Morenci toward the end of her pregnancy and go to California, where she gave birth to my sister Rebekah in Long Beach in 1913, to me in Hermosa Beach in 1915, and to my brother, Russell, in Santa Monica in 1919. Frances, my youngest sister, was born after we had settled in southern California.

The price of copper declined after World War I as did the Phelps Dodge Company itself. So in 1925 my parents decided to begin a new life in California, which was just beginning to boom. We headed for the area around the port of Los Angeles, which was a thriving rail and shipping terminal hard by major oil production and refining facilities. There was work here for an industrial surgeon, so my father moved us to nearby Wilmington, but practiced medicine in neighboring Long Beach and San Pedro since Wilmington had no hospital.

Growing up in a harbor town was a marvelous experience for a boy of ten. The place was a carnival of sailboats, yachts, oceangoing freighters, swaggering sailors, saloons, and mountains of dockside cargo amidst the smoke and smells of a busy shipping terminal. What it lacked was intellectual stimulation, since there were few professional people living there, and my schoolmates were infinitely more interested in finding a job, buying a car, and getting married than going on to college and a career.

I went to Wilmington High School and decided I wanted no part of medicine. Being trapped indoors all day and on call around the clock held no charm for me. I wanted to be a sportswriter. A tough, irreverent professional who writes like an angel and never misses a deadline. While I never reached those heights, I was sports editor of my high school newspaper, a high school sports columnist for the *Wilmington Press Journal*, and covered local Friday night sports events for the *Los Angeles Times*.

My father stimulated my interest in sports, which he religiously crammed into his hectic schedule during odd hours of the day or night. He taught me tennis, which I played at the old California Yacht Club, where I had been turned on to sailing and rowing. My father pushed me into golf by getting me up at 4:30 A.M., driving to the Palos Verdes Country Club in the fog, and playing four to six holes before breakfast. This would begin again in the evening when he'd drive me to a golf range in Long Beach for more practice. My father even had a three-hole putting green, complete with sandtrap, built in our back-yard. This helped him sharpen his game to the point where he was scoring in the seventies. Father was a very determined man, and I sometimes wish more of it had rubbed off on me. Instead I inherited my mother's calm demeanor and delight in simply putting things off.

But as I grew older, I realized that Father could not have led his nonstop life if it hadn't been for my mother. She was a hardworking woman who created the kind of comfortable home where he could catch his breath before roaring off again for another round of medicine or golf.

Mother's serenity was sorely tested when my father's mother came to live with us. She was a self-proclaimed aristocrat who arose early, dressed for breakfast, and expected to be waited on for the rest of the day. Mother somehow coped with this unexpected and demanding addition to her family, even finding time to garden, repair whatever needed fixing, and run the Beginners Nursery at our local Presbyterian church where we attended services every Sunday.

This was the 1930s and the Great Depression. Times were tough, and we may have been strapped financially, but if we were I never knew it. My sister Becky had entered the University of California at Los Angeles, and I followed her two years later. I was able to cut my living expenses to the bone by living with my mother's sister Pauline, who taught home economics at UCLA. It was 1933, I was eighteen, and I remember that my room, board, spending money, and tuition came to $40 a month.

I was majoring in journalism at UCLA when I decided to switch to medicine. My father never pushed me to follow in his footsteps, but something about his rewarding life as a doctor had obviously intrigued me. Little did I realize at the time that I was about to change from a carefree, girl-crazy journalism student with time on my hands to a student working day and night to master the basics of physics, chemistry, biology, and the rest of the premed curriculum. It was tough going. The competition for grades was awesome. But I loved every minute of it.

After graduating from UCLA, I began looking around for a good medical school, finally deciding on the University of Southern California. While my grades at UCLA had been good enough, they were far from brilliant, which caused me to approach my interview with the dean of the USC Medical School—Paul S. McKibben, M.D.—with something approaching fear and trembling. God forbid he should cross-examine me about the fundamentals of science.

When I walked into Dr. McKibben's office, I was delighted to see it was filled with sailing memorabilia. The dean was obviously a sailor, and it wasn't long before I learned he was the official timer for many of the races in which I had sailed. We spent the rest of the interview chatting about sailboat races in Los Angeles harbor without a single word being uttered about medicine or my academic record. A few days later, a letter arrived saying I had been accepted as a twenty-two-year-old medical student at Dr. McKibben's institution.

Learning to Be a Doctor

When I enrolled as a freshman at USC's Medical School in 1937, there were fifty-six students in my class, including two women (probably half would be women today). Quite a few medical schools begin classes with an intimidating orientation lecture in which you're told to "Look at the students on your left and right because by the end of the year one of them will be gone." The USC Medical School didn't work this way. Instead we were told, "The dean has handpicked you and he doesn't like to be wrong, so it's up to the faculty to keep you in school."

This was my kind of school, but it was a rough grind nevertheless. We went to classes six days a week, studied six nights a week, and I doubt I could have made it if it hadn't been for Saturday night, when we metamorphosed into party animals dedicated to forgetting about medicine until the beer ran out. What girlfriends I had also ran out when they realized I would be devoted to a monastic life of virtually nonstop studying for the next four years.

I began by living at home and commuting to school. But I felt isolated because I had to study alone. So I decided to move into the Nu Sigma Nu medical fraternity house on campus, which raised both my spirits and my grades. As I delved deeper into medicine, I realized I wanted to be a doer and not a thinker, which led me inexorably to surgery. It could have been the subconscious influence of my father and my uncle Jewell Smith, who were both surgeons, or maybe it was simply my lifetime interest in gadgets, tools, and things mechanical.

When my classmates and I reached our senior year in 1941, the war in Europe was well under way and many of the doctors at the massive Los Angeles County General Hospital were called to active military service leaving it short of physicians. We were pressed into service as junior interns to fill the gap, and before long we considered ourselves to be real-life doctors with the confidence and self-assurance to match, which stayed with us for the rest of our medical lives.

The day I graduated from USC and received my medical degree was filled with the usual sadness at leaving classmates I might never see again, and the pure joy of realizing that my years of nonstop medical education were finished. But there was something more, something which would later prove to be of even greater importance to me than my hard-won medical degree. For out there among the thousands of students graduating that day from USC's various colleges was a young woman I had never met. Little did I realize we would shortly be together for the rest of our lives.

I became an intern at the huge Los Angeles County General Hospital in July 1941, and planned to stay there for the next two years. One of my fellow interns was Dick Barton, who had married while we were in medical school and wanted me to meet a young lady named Kathleen Hambly, who had been his wife, Patty's, roommate at the Pi

Phi sorority house on the USC campus when we were all students there. So one Sunday afternoon I borrowed my family's Cadillac and the four of us went off to a tea dance at the Mission Inn in nearby Riverside. I saw a great deal of Miss Hambly from that moment until we were married a short time later.

It was nothing for interns back then to work all day, all night, and all day again. That was the routine. But we didn't care because we were young and wanted to learn. I'd grab some sleep when I could, some food when I could, and that habit has stayed with me. I still get fidgety if I have to sit at a dinner table too long, and usually don't care what I eat, or worse, don't know what I've eaten, which annoys my wife after she's gone to the trouble of preparing a delicious meal. Interns today are paid decent salaries, work fewer hours a day, and rotate weekends and nights on call. It's another world.

I was making the rounds on LA County General's neurosurgical ward at 10 A.M. on December 7, 1941, when some patients listening to their radio headsets yelled, "The Japanese have just bombed Pearl Harbor." I didn't think much about it, and was soon on my way out of the hospital to pick up Kit, and then grab a few things from a bakery so we could have brunch with friends. We talked about the bombing, which seemed far away, not realizing that it would soon change all our lives, and the lives of those around us.

There was a virtual overnight roundup and deportation of Japanese doctors, nurses, and interns—along with our gardener—since they were highly visible, and it was thought wise to protect them from possible retaliation. Next came the military call-up of many of our hospital's other doctors and nurses, followed by a parade of war-related events from blackouts to gas rationing to food stamps.

My most memorable experience at LA County General happened exactly one year later on the night of December 7, 1942, when the people of Los Angeles thought they saw a Japanese plane flying around overhead. Wartime searchlights were turned on. Antiaircraft guns began firing. Everybody switched off their house lights. Stones were thrown at any street lamps still left burning. And cars kept moving even though their headlights were off, creating a ghastly bonanza for our hospital.

Panicky people were running down the dark streets. Cars with no lights would hit them just below the knees causing what we call "bumper fractures." I was on duty that night, and I went up to the hospital's sixteenth floor roof to watch the excitement. I stayed there until the all clear was sounded after someone decided the Japanese plane was a false alarm. I expected casualties to pour into the hospital. But instead it was very quiet, with no one showing up at our emergency room. The reason was that the ambulances weren't running because the streetlights hadn't been turned back on. But then the lights came on, ambulances began picking up everyone who had been hurt, and we were flooded with accident victims. It was awesome. We worked around the clock until hundreds of people with all kinds of injuries had been treated.

Coast Guard Lieutenant

My fellow interns at LA County General Hospital were eagerly joining one of the three services, and because I loved the sea I decided to join the Navy, which promptly rejected me because of an old high school basketball injury. I had just passed the U.S. Air Force examination when a Coast Guard recruiter came to the hospital and said they were building up their medical department and needed doctors. I saw this as my second chance to go to sea and was commissioned a lieutenant on August 20, 1942.

I started out by giving induction physicals to prospective sailors in Los Angeles and later in Long Beach. I was then transferred to Lompoc, California, to provide regional medical coverage for men patrolling the coastline in the Santa Barbara area, as well as those flying overhead in blimps on antisubmarine patrol. This was not far from a place I'd be spending a lot of my time more than forty years later—President Ronald Reagan's California ranch.

Since I was now earning $135 a month—the most money I had made in my life—I decided it was time to ask Kit for her hand in marriage. We had started making plans to be married near my Coast Guard station in Santa Barbara when orders arrived moving me to the San Diego air station. This move put our wedding day on hold, but not for long. Kit and I were married shortly thereafter in a small church in Pasadena followed by a reception at the Jonathan Club in Los Angeles. We had planned to honeymoon at the Grand Canyon, and since I was in uniform I was able to get a round-trip ticket, while the best she could do was one-way. We spent most of our honeymoon at the Grand Canyon railroad station until we succeeded in getting her a ticket back home to San Diego.

Kit was attractive, witty, resourceful, intelligent, and a wonderful friend during those difficult wartime days. Her father's family had arrived in California via Britain and Canada, while her mother's family had come from Virginia and Ohio. Kit was born and grew up in Los Angeles, and went on to the University of Southern California, where she was elected to the Phi Beta Kappa academic honor society, named all-around woman of the year as a senior, and crowned "Helen of Troy" homecoming queen for the University of Southern California Trojans.

We thoroughly enjoyed married life in San Diego even though the bay was filled with ships and the trappings of war. It wasn't long before seven large ships arrived from the East Coast, and I was assigned to one of them as the junior medical officer among five doctors and a dentist. We were to begin training with U.S. Marines from nearby Camp Pendleton as part of an amphibious landing unit headed for combat in the South Pacific.

Our ship was designated an APA (auxiliary personnel assault) which meant we carried a battalion-sized landing team that would assault the beach on an enemy island and take it over. I was assigned as the beach party medical officer which meant I would go ashore with the fourth landing wave, establish an aid-station on the beach to accept battle casualties, and then put them aboard small landing craft which would transfer them to ships offshore where they'd receive definitive care. Little did I realize at the time that this was ideal training for someone destined to become physician to the president of the United States.

One night we left San Diego loaded with thousands of Marines, cruised all night, and began a practice landing on the beach north of San Diego at Las Pulgus Canyon. My medical beach party consisted of twelve corpsmen and myself, and since we were not scheduled to land until the fourth wave I was very relaxed. That is, until I learned the fourth wave would hit the beach exactly four minutes after the first.

It wasn't long before our ship was involved in its first attack against Kwajalein, a Japanese-held atoll in the Pacific. It was a night landing where we rendezvoused out at sea and then dashed for the beach at the crack of dawn, landing there before the troops arrived. This was kind of frightening because, among other things, I didn't know how to defend myself against the enemy. So I went to my superior, a Captain Treadway, and said, "Sir, we need some training on how to fight for our lives if attacked." "Doctor," he replied, "you just concentrate on being a doctor, and leave the fighting to us." I ran into this mind-set forty years later when I started working at the White House, wanted to discuss some political ideas I had, and was told by a presidential assistant, "We'll take care of the politics, and you just be a doctor."

In the beginning, we doctors were protected by nothing more than Red Cross patches on our uniforms and helmets, and our hospital ships by huge red crosses on their decks and sides which could be seen at night since they always had their lights blazing and music blaring. That was until one of them was bombed by a Japanese kamikaze. After that, the hospital ships ran at night without lights, and I was given an Army Colt .45 revolver which nobody ever taught me how to use.

I spent the rest of 1944 hitting the beaches on the Japanese-held islands of Emiru, Saipan, Guam, Palau, and Leyte Gulf in the Philippines. There were five doctors and a dentist on my transport ship, and since I was the youngest, I, together with several of my corpsmen, was assigned to cover a section of the beach while the remaining doctors stayed aboard the ship as surgeons (as did the dentist who also served as anaesthesiologist).

My job was to treat men injured by bullets, blasts from exploding artillery shells, heavy ammunition boxes falling on their hands, Jeeps running over their feet, and other medical problems I had never seen before including incoherent shell-shocked soldiers who staggered down to the beach endangering themselves and their buddies.

My only supplies as beach party medical officer were those for emergency care that my corpsmen and I carried on our backs: intravenous solutions, blood plasma, dressings, and so forth. My job was to give first aid to men I thought had a chance of surviving, and then evacuate them to the assault ships waiting offshore. This was a terrible business because I had to play God, deciding, at sundown, which injured men would be sent back to the assault ships, and which would be left there on the beach perhaps to die before the ships returned in the morning.

The Japanese succeeded in holding us down on the beach on Saipan, eventually driving us off the beach until the Navy's guns and aircraft were able to knock out their firepower so we could return to our beachhead. The Japanese allowed us to land troops and supplies on the beach at Saipan on the morning of June 15, 1944, but started lobbing shells at us in the afternoon. The atolls we had captured before were flat which meant we could land on one side at eight o'clock in the morning, and then fight our way to the other side by midafternoon. But Saipan was different. It had a hill in the middle packed with Japanese whose mortars were trained on the beach.

I thought my medical unit would be on the beach for three days before the Marines dislodged the heavily dug-in Japanese. But it was more than three weeks before the Marines were able to control the island, set up regular hospitals on the beach, and allow us to return to our ship for a rest after treating as many as several hundred injured men in a single day. Japanese fighter planes from the nearby island of Guam strafed us up and down the beach on the night of D day plus three. Two Marine patients on either side of me were killed, but we held our beachhead even as shells were screaming over our heads.

It was a great relief to return to our ship, take a hot shower, change into clean clothes, and find a stack of letters waiting for me from Kit (including one with the news that we had become the parents of a baby girl named Deanne born five days before the invasion of Saipan). It was at moments like this that I felt alone, far away from the ones I loved, yet convinced that I would eventually return home to Kit and our growing family, even though nothing is certain during wartime.

I was in on General Douglas MacArthur's return to the Philippines on October 25, 1944, when an assault team of 225,000 men landed at Leyte Gulf. Once we were on the beach, and a large beachhead was secured, the Army did something new by immediately converting a number of the big landing ships into hospital ships, each with a speciality such as burns, general medicine, orthopedics, neurosurgery, psychiatrics, and trauma, which worked out very well.

After that I returned to Guam, which we had taken from the Japanese, to rehearse for what we felt would be an unusually bloody landing on the heavily fortified island of Iwo Jima 750 miles south of Tokyo set for February 18, 1945. It was kind of a rule of thumb that after you had made five landings your number was about up. So before I could participate in my sixth landing on Iwo, I was reassigned to the U.S. Marine Hospital in San Francisco.

I still remember the thrill of seeing the Golden Gate Bridge as we steamed into San Francisco, and immediately getting a leave so I could join Kit and Deanne Hambly Smith, who was now ten months old. We quickly found an apartment and were comfortably tucked in when Germany surrendered on May 7, 1945, followed by Japan's capitulation on September 2, 1945. This ended a gnawing fear of mine that I might be assigned to participate in the invasion of Japan, which some intelligence estimates concluded might cost up to a million Allied casualties.

The war was finally over, and my work at the Marine hospital consisted of performing discharge physical examinations and evaluating duty-related injury and illness for service-connected disability. My own time in the service was about up, and in February 1945, I took a month's discharge leave so Kit, the baby, and I could return to my parents' home in Wilmington, California, where I started working for my father as a general practitioner. I had been out of uniform for a month when my official discharge from the U.S. Coast Guard came through on March 12, 1946.

I'd decided that after the war I'd go into orthopedics, which has to do with bone fractures. I'm a mechanically minded kind of person, and I liked the gadgetry, the surgery, the X-ray work, and the fact that if somebody breaks his leg you fix it and it's done (although they all don't always work out that way).

But when I was in San Francisco, one of my doctor buddies was a urologist who had completed his urological training at the Johns Hopkins Hospital in Baltimore; he was naturally very enthusiastic about his speciality, which involves the study of the kidneys, ureter, and bladder (plus the penis and scrotum in men). This is a very small, compact little package where we have great diagnostic tools allowing us to x-ray, measure, look at, and test, so that it's rare when you can't make a diagnosis in urology, which comforted me a lot. What's more, when you've got a problem, you can do something about it. If it's kidney stones, you can take them out. Prostate problems—you can correct with surgery. If it's cancer, you're pretty much beaten, but not as much today as before because more people are having regular checkups.

I had never considered urology, but began to when my friend Dr. John Haines kept insisting that "the casualties suffered in World War II are going to produce thousands of orthopedists who are expert at setting broken bones. But it won't produce any urologists because young soldiers don't have many urological problems to treat."

Then I ran into an amazing person in San Francisco named Dr. Leo Elowesser, who was a renowned chest surgeon. I was interested in chest surgery, which deals mainly with tuberculosis, tumors, emphysema, and cancer. It is a kind of messy, end-of-the-line business. My father counseled me that practically every chest patient you see has been ill for years, and the results of treating them are very poor and unrewarding.

Talked into Becoming a Urologist

I thought any medical field was interesting provided it generated a lot of surgery, which is why I decided against psychiatry, dermatology, delivering babies, and the like (although delivering babies is fun because at least you get a slap on the back from their parents). I had no particular interest in urology either, but my urologist pal eventually talked me into it. I ended up being interviewed by Dr. David M. Davis, a professor of urology who had just left Johns Hopkins and was teaching at the Thomas Jefferson Medical College Hospital in Philadelphia.

When I was studying medicine in California, I kept hearing what outstanding medical events were taking place at Massachusetts General, at Johns Hopkins, and at the Mayo Clinic. It all seemed to come from East to West. So I decided to go East, accepting a three-year residency at Jefferson to work and study urology. Kit and I packed the car with our few possessions, cleaned out our meager bank account, gathered up our baby daughter, and headed for the City of Brotherly Love.

I reported to the Jefferson Medical College Hospital on a Sunday night, and was greeted by Dr. Manny Lubin, the urological resident, who said, "Welcome to 'Jeff'; my father's just had a heart attack and I'm leaving for Oklahoma." I stood there in shock, but managed to blurt out, "Show me where I meet Dr. Davis tomorrow" before retrieving my little family waiting in the car and moving them into a room in the Benjamin Franklin Hotel located across the street from the hospital. It wasn't long before Kit had found some temporary rooms with a family living nearby, and as she looked after our new home and baby I worked from sunup to sundown learning how to treat people with urological problems.

Our living expenses were considerable, and the $135 a month I received under the G.I. bill had to be supplemented by our parents since I received nothing for being a resident doctor my first year, nothing my second year, and only $35 a month the third year. But, here again, to be a good doctor you must pay for the privilege of training at good hospitals. And I was lucky enough to study under Dr. Davis, who was a very intellectual, innovative surgeon, and I think some of this spilled over onto me in the course of pursuing what was to become my life's profession.

Our son Turner was born in October 1946, and by this time we had better living conditions in a parklike setting near Philadelphia's Schuylkill River. Time passed quickly at Jefferson, and by my last year there I was "king of the hill." There was no surgical procedure I couldn't handle. I was in demand and respected by the rest of the hospital's staff, thanks to the marvelous teaching and guidance I had received from Dr. Davis and his fellow doctors at "Jeff."

Kit and I were eager to get back to California as soon as my three years were up at Jefferson. This worked out well since there weren't any openings in Philadelphia for young urologists anyway. In fact, there were only about thirty-five urological residencies in the entire country at that time, versus about 130 today (although the profession is clearly overgrown and efforts are currently under way to reduce it to more reasonable levels).

Dr. Davis was appalled that I was returning to southern California with no job lined up. But it didn't bother me at all since I believed that if you want to be completely happy, you should go where you want to live and worry about practicing later. So one hour after I had finished my grand rounds on Saturday, we piled in the car and headed for Los Angeles, which would always be home for us.

When I returned to California I was known as a "Philadelphia specialist," which wasn't all bad. Nor was the fact that I was a urological surgeon, since there were so few of us back then. I was lucky to have been trained to treat internal problems such as kidney stones, kidney tumors, obstructive kidneys, bladder difficulties, prostate trouble, and all diseases of the urinary tract. Most urologists at that time knew only about gonorrhea and syphilis, and when penicillin came along in 1944 it changed all that, essentially wiping out gonorrhea. Suddenly all those "clap" doctors were rushing to become urological surgeons, which was kind of pathetic because they hadn't been trained for it.

Building My Practice

The Los Angeles we returned to in 1949 was expanding in every direction at once, making it difficult to decide where we wanted to live and build my practice. I knew I had to be near a hospital since I was a surgical specialist, and after looking around for three months we decided on the west side of Los Angeles.

Kit and I rented a house, and I started practicing urology in nearby Beverly Hills, which was great even though it didn't have a hospital because there was an ordinance against having one. Consequently I sent my patients downtown to Good Samaritan Hospital, California Hospital, Methodist Hospital, Santa Monica Hospital, and Saint John's Hospital. The trouble was, I never seemed to be where I was needed. When I was at my office I was needed at a hospital. And when I was at a hospital I was needed back at the office. However, the traffic in Los Angeles was tolerable then, so I managed.

One day in Beverly Hills, I ran into Dr. Lloyd Stirrett, a university classmate of mine who was working at the long-established, highly regarded Nelson Clinic. The clinic had no particular urologist on its staff, so I began doing all its urological work, which helped me immensely in getting started. Soon I was sharing an office with Dr. Gilbert Thomas, who was well-known in urological circles. I was much younger than Dr. Thomas, and could have worked as his assistant. But Dr. Davis, my urology professor at Jefferson Hospital in Philadelphia, had told me, "I have trained you well. You can compete with anybody in the country and you must stand on your own two feet. If you feel you need financial help, call me and I will send you money to tide you over."

So I started building my own practice, just as my office colleague Dr. Thomas was building his. Soon referrals started coming in from other doctors, although few from my old California medical school classmates who had said, "Oh you're here now; we'll keep you busy." But I never heard boo from them. With referrals it's just a matter of being around and getting to know people. You have to keep working at it, and back then we didn't advertise like doctors can today.

I became a consultant to the Veterans Administration because of my military experience, and usually went over there to consult and teach two or three times a week. I was paid $25 per visit, which wasn't much, but it helped. I also had an occasional patient from the Nelson Clinic, and my wife recommended me to a few of her friends. I was spread pretty thin. But I needed to support my family, which continued to grow with my daughter Christine's arrival in 1950.

As my practice grew, it became increasingly difficult for me to cover the patients I regularly sent to five different hospitals. So I started looking for one hospital to associate with and found it one hot summer afternoon after leaving downtown Los Angeles and driving west on Wilshire Boulevard to Santa Monica and its refreshing ocean breezes. At that moment I decided to settle in Santa Monica and use Saint John's as my primary hospital.

Saint John's Hospital was reasonably new, and had been created by the Sisters of Charity of Leavenworth, Kansas, who owned and managed it. It was a clean, calm, and competent place to practice medicine and it remains so to this day. I had much in common with most of Saint John's staff doctors, who had been World War II specialists like myself. The Veterans Hospital was also nearby, and there were plans to develop a medical school as part of the University of California at Los Angeles. Also, there was the Pacific Ocean, which has been part of my life since I was a youngster, plus the fact that this area seemed destined to become Los Angeles's most affluent suburb. All of this made it an ideal place for a young doctor with a growing family to put down his roots.

What I didn't realize, of course, was that I had unwittingly put myself on a course that would allow me to cross paths with Ronald Reagan and the White House. My decision to become a medical doctor, to specialize in urology, to return to Los Angeles from Philadelphia, to live on the west side of town, and to practice surgery at Saint John's Hospital positioned me to meet Ronald Reagan.

Ronald Reagan, on the other hand, had gone into the entertainment field, worked his way to Los Angeles, decided to live on the west side of Los Angeles, and used Saint John's Hospital for his family's medical care.

Thus, we ran a parallel course and because of his urological illness in 1966 and my being called to diagnose and treat him, our paths crossed and we established a medical relationship that endured until 1985 when I was called to be of medical service to him under very different conditions, for a different reason, and some 3,000 miles from our homes: to be his White House physician.

Chapter Four

Getting Started in the White House

The first thing I learned after leaving private practice to become White House physician to the president of the United States was "Never keep him waiting." There are, however, times when you can't help yourself. Dr. John Hutton, my assistant, locked himself in a bathroom when President Reagan was giving the commencement address at the U.S. Naval Academy, which delayed the departure of the presidential motorcade. I took this "Never keep the president waiting" rule very seriously whenever I was scheduled to join Ronald Reagan for an early morning motorcade in Washington, or a trip outside the capital aboard Air Force One. I'd set my alarm clock at home. I would also ask the staff to ring me well before departure time on my private White House telephone. I'd tell the White House driver who was picking me up to bang on my door if I wasn't waiting for him. And I'd always wake up at least an hour early anyway.

But I, too, broke the sacred rule within days after coming to Washington when I was still a greenhorn. It happened on January 21, 1985, shortly after President Reagan had given his second, and last, inaugural address inside the Capitol rotunda on a bitter cold day when Washington was blanketed with snow.

Kit and I had left our Watergate apartment together; she took a special bus to the rotunda, while I was driven directly to my office in the White House basement. I waited outside the office as President Reagan, Mrs. Reagan, and the inaugural party came down from the living quarters and walked briskly through the Diplomatic Reception Room and out into his waiting limousine. The presidential motorcade moved slowly through the White House gates, and turned eastward toward the Capitol.

The scene was incredible. Dazzling white, but with an eerie empti-

43

ness. No cars. No people. Just blocks of empty and forlorn snow-covered bleachers which should have been packed with happy, cheering people as the president's motorcade passed by on the way to the Capitol.

The motorcade entered the Capitol basement driveway, where President Reagan was met by the speaker of the House and Senate majority leader. I and other White House staff members were taken to House Speaker Thomas "Tip" O'Neill's office, which served as a holding room, and after a short wait were escorted to the rotunda. I scanned the guests awaiting the president's arrival, looking for Kit, and finally spotted her standing next to Barbara Bush—two white-haired ladies whose heads could be seen clearly on the following week's cover of *Time* magazine featuring the Reagan inaugural.

President Reagan entered the rotunda, as the Marine Band played "Hail to the Chief," and walked directly to the podium to give his inaugural address. The president then left for the traditional luncheon hosted by members of Congress, and afterwards was escorted back to Tip O'Neill's office jammed with congressional well-wishers.

I waited outside to join the president for the ten- or twelve-minute motorcade back to the White House. But he and his party left through one exit as I stood by another. I figured something was wrong when it suddenly became deathly quiet. I rushed for the motorcade, which was already moving, and was hauled aboard one of the last cars by the president's advance man Jim Kuhn. The presidential motorcade really moves. Everybody runs for limousines, and it seems like seconds later the motorcade is gone.

I had been looking forward to riding in the inaugural parade down Pennsylvania Avenue. Nearly a dozen members of my family had flown to Washington to share my moment of glory. But it was not to be as the subfreezing weather forced the cancellation of the first inaugural parade since 1833 when Andrew Jackson was sworn into office.

The head of public health in the district was worried about the icy streets and the wind-chill factor, which at one point hit eleven degrees below zero, and when he asked me if the parade should be called off I told him the president would be very unhappy if the weather hurt anybody during the ceremony. I had visions of drum majorettes up from sunny Florida getting frostbite on their bare legs and horn players having their instruments freeze to their lips. Professionally I was relieved when the parade was canceled. Personally for me, and most of the country, it was a heartbreaking decision.

Press reports told how sixty-six floats standing by at a warehouse in the Washington Navy Yard were torn apart when word came through that there wasn't going to be a parade. One of the last floats to go was to have carried eighty-five members of an a cappella choir from the Aberdeen Central High School in South Dakota down Pennsylvania Avenue, and past the presidential reviewing stand. The students had raised $12,000 to build the float, and the townspeople of Aberdeen had chipped in another $40,000 to send them to Washington. Sadly, in the end they had to settle for having their picture taken on the float before it was destroyed.

Street vendors who had stocked up on inauguration souvenirs lost their shirts. Companies throwing catered parties in hotel suites along the parade route ended up donating the gourmet food to shelters for the homeless. And the Presidential Inaugural Committee was faced with having to refund $800,000 to some 25,000 people who had paid between $12.50 and $100 for curbside seats to watch the festivities in comfort.

The president and First Lady invited all 12,000 people who were scheduled to be in the inaugural parade to join them for a celebration at the Capital Centre in nearby Landover, Maryland. They thanked them all, told them how disappointed they were that they couldn't see them all perform, and then looked on as several of the dozens of marching bands which had traveled to Washington to do their stuff performed one brief number apiece. Kit and I did get to attend several inaugural balls, galas, and other festivities, along with being there when President Reagan gave his inaugural address in the Capitol rotunda.

It was during these first days in the White House that I came to appreciate today's security which surrounds recent presidents of the United States compared with those who held that high office in days gone by.

President Abraham Lincoln, according to a contemporary account, knew "that incitements to murder him were not uncommon in the South." Yet he "would walk at midnight, with a single secretary or alone, from the Executive Mansion to the War Department, and back. He would ride through the lonely roads of an uninhabited suburb from the White House to the Soldiers' Home in the dusk of evening, and return to his work in the morning before the town was astir. He was greatly annoyed when, late in the war, it was decided that there must be a guard stationed at the Executive Mansion, and that a squad of cavalry must accompany him on his daily ride; but he was always reasonable and yielded to the best judgments of others."

Modern American presidents are much better protected than the Great Emancipator, and nowhere is this more evident than in the steel cocoon which surrounds them everywhere they go, otherwise known as the presidential motorcade. I was astonished shortly after I arrived in Washington when I had to get into a motorcade taking the president to see an exhibit of pictures by chief White House photographer Michael Evans at the Corcoran Gallery of Art which is clearly visible from the White House Lawn. The president could have strolled there in forty-five seconds.

President Reagan's Motorcade

President Reagan's typical motorcade was led by a police car from the local community—in the capital it was the Metropolitan Washington Police—with its lights flashing and an officer behind the wheel who knew exactly where the president was going, as does the White House advance man sitting next to him who has gone over the route several times and is familiar with every turn, every corner.

Motorcycle police ride along both sides of the motorcade, with one group zooming ahead to clear an approaching intersection and then dropping back, while a second group rushes forward to clear the next one. They keep changing places, giving the president an ear-to-ear grin each time they roar past his limousine.

Washington crowds wave furiously every time a big, black heavily armored limousine speeds by with the presidential seal on the sides, flags waving from its two front fenders, and usually two presidential aides in the back seat who everyone takes for the president and the First Lady. As the motorcade roars past, men generally stand there, while women more often jump up and down and frantically wave their arms. I drew this striking fact to the attention of the White House staffers who rode with me, and from then on it was referred to as "Smith's Law."

If the president was attending an affair with a head of state or other dignitary, an "augmented" motorcade would be formed with a special limousine inserted in front of the president's car for the First Lady and the dignitary's spouse.

President Reagan usually sat on the right side of his limousine behind his top Secret Service bodyguard, Ray Shaddick. The car was driven by another armed Secret Service agent who had been thoroughly trained to take evasive action in the event of a shootout.

One of the cars in the motorcade held four Secret Service agents who would jump out and surround the president's limousine whenever it stopped or slowed down. Another agent with a machine gun sat in the back seat facing the rear in case the president's limousine was attacked from behind.

There's a van in the motorcade, known as the Combat Attack Team, or CAT, car, which holds a heavily armed SWAT team dressed in black. Its job is to protect the president if an unidentified vehicle suddenly careens toward the president's limousine or if terrorists dart out from the crowd carrying guns, grenades, bazookas, or anything else that's deadly. The president's limousine would take evasive action, and the SWAT team would go after whoever was threatening his life.

A key vehicle in every presidential motorcade is the Control Car, with the military aide toting the "football" sitting up front with an Army driver wearing a chauffeur's uniform. The aide controls all communications to and from the motorcade, with those involving the president routed through the Secret Service man sitting next to the limousine driver. I'd be in the back seat with other White House staffers who would change from time to time depending on the makeup of the motorcade, or when we weren't riding with the president. Advance man Bill Henkle was often with us, and when we were headed toward a political rally or similar event he would get calls from people at the site telling him about the size and mood of the crowd which he'd telephone up to the president's car if there was something interesting to report.

Toward the end of the motorcade were cars holding another advance person, the head of the president's military office, and my nurse, who never rode with me so that one of us would survive to care for the president in the event of a catastrophic shootout.

Finally came the press vans filled with reporters including one or more with "death watch" television cameras protruding from their roofs so they could film the entire motorcade from start to finish. The camera was there to avoid what happened in Dallas, Texas, where the only film record of the killing of President John F. Kennedy was a color home movie taken by a local dress manufacturer named Abraham Zapruder. The footage of that home movie is at the heart of the controversy swirling around the Kennedy assassination, which is debated even to this day.

There was always an ambulance in the motorcade to evacuate the wounded in case of a shootout or accident. It was manned by a rotating team of specially trained police paramedics whose security could not be cleared in advance. An armed Secret Service agent was assigned to ride along with them.

Bringing up the rear was another police car with its lights flashing as the motorcade whizzed by. Flying overhead was an armed helicopter often called "gunboat," guarding the president from on high.

Trying to Please the President

An illustration of this was during the president's trip to Quebec, Canada, on March 17 and 18, 1985, for talks with Prime Minister Brian Mulroney. We stayed at the lovely old Château Frontenac Hotel. The hotel's management wanted to make a good impression, so they painted the entire floor containing the presidential suite. This proved to be a minidisaster for the Reagans, who spent a restless night enveloped in obnoxious fumes. My room was next to theirs, and I could hear them struggling to open the windows all night as I was wheezing and tossing myself. From that moment on, Rick Ahern and his advance people, who checked things out before the president's arrival, lived according to "Ahern's Law," which stated, "Never paint a room right before the president of the United States is going to sleep in it."

Shortly after I returned from Quebec, I received the first of six certificates of appreciation signed by President Reagan which he gave to everyone who accompanied him on his trips abroad and helped make them go off without a hitch. These certificates now hang on the wall of my study at home, and are pleasant reminders of the times I was with the president on trips to Quebec, Canada; the island of Grenada in the Caribbean; Bonn, West Germany, with side trips to Spain and Portugal; Geneva, Switzerland; the Indonesian island of Bali; Tokyo, Japan; and, finally, Reykjavík, Iceland.

The Trauma of Taking Orders

My new job meant I had to learn to take orders, which isn't easy for doctors, particularly those of my generation. I lived in the era when I was the boss, and I got a little tired of third-party intervention, peer review groups, or some secretary telling me what to do. I was not used to that.

One man who did not hesitate to give me direct orders was the president's top Secret Service aide, Ray Shaddick, who, with three other agents, was never more than a few feet from the president in what Ray called the "kill zone." Ray told me to stay well outside the "kill zone" so that if the president were shot I'd be safe and could rush to his side and try to save his life.

I remember President Reagan was giving a speech on tax reform in Oshkosh, Wisconsin, when someone in the crowd fainted from the heat. The president saw what had happened, and interrupted his speech to ask if anyone needed a doctor, pointing directly at me. I started to move toward the person who had fainted, when Major Robert Ivany, the president's military aide, grabbed me and said, "Don't move. This could be a ploy to distract you by someone who plans to hurt the president." I was distracted a few minutes later by three coeds from the University of Wisconsin who had stripped to the waist, jumped on the shoulders of three husky guys, and unfurled a protest banner. Later in the day I asked the president if he had seen this memorable demonstration and he assured me he had not.

I also goofed following a lunch for the president at the State Department hosted by Secretary of State George Shultz. After lunch, Secretary Shultz wanted to ride down in the elevator with us to the basement, where the presidential motorcade was waiting. The elevator was packed wall-to-wall with the president's party so I got off to make room for him. When I rejoined the president several minutes later in the basement, I was reprimanded by Jim Kuhn for having left the president's side. "Suppose the elevator had gotten stuck," said Kuhn, "and the president had suffered a heart attack and desperately needed you?" He was right, of course, and I never made that mistake again.

I got into trouble again following the first physical examination given to President Reagan under my supervision on March 8, 1985, at the Naval Hospital in Bethesda. I had finished as much of the exam as I could in my White House medical office, and already had the data on his height and weight, the results of his blood and urine tests, plus an electrocardiogram of his heart. I wanted to know what the risk factors were before the president arrived at Bethesda. By doing this, I could be sure that everything would go boom, boom, boom, and I wouldn't have to waste a minute of the president's time.

We flew to Bethesda on the president's helicopter, Marine One, and no sooner had its door opened than the press started shouting questions at the Reagans about the president's health. "On a scale of one to ten he's an eleven," Mrs. Reagan shouted back as she strode across the lawn toward the hospital with the Reagan's sheepdog Lucky tugging on his leash. Presidential press spokesman Larry Speakes added that Mr. Reagan was "healthy as a horse," and that the examination was purely routine.

The examination began in the presidential suite, where I had the bed moved aside so we could bring in a treadmill. I had Mr. Reagan change into a pair of navy blue warm-up pants and tennis shoes, stuck electronic leads on his chest which were hooked up to an electrocardiogram machine, and then had him walk vigorously on the treadmill for about ten minutes. I gave him this stress test to check for cardiac irregularities, or coronary artery disease. President Reagan took the test as a personal challenge, did much better than most men his age, and gave us no cause for alarm.

I had arranged for the checkup to be conducted by a team of six distinguished doctors headed by Navy Captain Walter W. Karney, a specialist in internal medicine, backed up by Dr. Edward Cattau, a gastroenterologist, plus two of my assistants, Colonel John Hutton and Lieutenant Commander Kenneth Lee. The process took three hours and involved a battery of tests in addition to the electrocardiogram, ranging from an eye exam to a chest X ray, and showed seventy-four-year-old President Reagan to be in good health. The only negative was a small polyp we discovered in his lower colon which was biopsied and proved to be noncancerous. Dr. Cattau felt it didn't have to be removed immediately but could wait until July when the president returned from attending an economic summit meeting in Bonn, West Germany.

When I had finished the exam, presidential press spokesman Larry Speakes's deputy Mark Weinberg came to my office and said, "Now, let's have all the results." So I said, "Fine," thinking he and Larry would cull them over and put out what they thought was proper. So I enumerated everything, and they repeated it all to the entire Washington press corps. The *New York Times* ran the story under a two-column headline on page one, then jumped it to an inside page where it was spread across five columns with nothing left out.

From there on we agreed to talk to the family first since the family has a right to consultation and privacy.

I could not have agreed more. All my medical life I have been a strict advocate of respecting doctor-patient confidentiality. My wife's close friends were amazed and hurt that she did not know I was taking care of them because I never told her. So Nancy Reagan was correct, and I learned a lesson about handling news in the White House. I suddenly became very guarded when being debriefed by Speakes and Weinberg, providing them with just enough information to meet the public's right to know.

Nancy Reagan is not the kind of person you get to know on a thigh-slapping basis, and I rarely saw her relax even though on one notable occasion she did let her hair down enough to have some fun at her own expense. The First Lady was known for her love of high-fashion clothes, and at the annual Gridiron Dinner in 1982, where top journalists poke fun at the president and he pokes back, she brought the house down and I'm sure stunned the president. The First Lady of the land suddenly appeared on the stage as part of the evening's entertainment wearing a garish blue flowered skirt, an even more outrageous red flowered blouse, a moth-eaten white feather boa slung carelessly around her neck, a big red Chinese coolie-type hat, and yellow rain boots as she sang, "I'm wearing secondhand clothes, secondhand clothes," to the tune of "Secondhand Rose."

Shortly after I arrived at the White House, I met with her, laid out the various ways I planned to look after her husband's health, and asked her if she was happy with this approach, if things were being run the way she wanted them.

"What Do You Give a President?"

We've always given gifts in our family, but decided it would be wrong to give the president something personal because he was my boss and it just didn't seem right. It wasn't long, however, before we found that so many people did give him gifts that we felt a little negligent. We sent the Reagans a card the first Christmas we were in Washington, but the following year we sent them a beautiful handmade metallic-gray flower basket from California with a huge gray lead bow which Kit filled with showy white cyclamen plants. The First Lady liked it so much she put it on a table in the main hall of their residence. It wasn't long before it was seen by the official White House flower arranger, who ordered a dozen to decorate an official state dinner. We also gave the president several jars of nut-roca bars which he liked, and he and Mrs. Reagan gave us a set of water glasses with the presidential seal and his name etched on them.

Doctor's Wife in Washington

Kit had a wonderful time during her two years in Washington. Our apartment was close to George Washington University, and she thought she'd go there to perfect her Spanish and resume her piano lessons. Then she realized she was living in the middle of a whole panorama of our country's museums, monuments, and historical places and had four wonderful days a week to drink them in before joining me for our Friday afternoon weekend trips to Camp David with the Reagans.

Kit was soon caught up in seeing the sights around the capital, attending charity luncheons, playing tennis with newfound Washington friends, and joining me for presidential receptions, State Department dinners, arrival ceremonies for foreign heads of state, and other occasions.

Christmas in the White House

The First Lady is the president's hostess in the White House, and we were continually amazed by the warm, friendly, and unpretentious way she arranged the social events held in what for eight years was her home. She approved in advance all the menus for official White House dinners along with the ambiance which surrounded them. I remember one Christmas season when the theme was Mother Goose nursery rhymes, and another when it was an old-fashioned Christmas featuring dolls dressed up in winter clothes ice-skating, sledding, throwing snowballs, building snowmen, and enjoying other winter activities.

The one responsible for this artistry was Nancy Clark, the head of White House decorations and flower arranging. She dreamed up designs for the flowers, plants, and trees, but she would always take her ideas upstairs for Mrs. Reagan's approval before proceeding.

Their greatest triumph, I think, was the way they decorated the White House on March 18, 1986, for the state dinner honoring Canadian Prime Minister Brian Mulroney. The National Park Service took cherry trees and wrapped the branches with hundreds of miniature white lights. The trees were then placed in a hothouse where the white, double-blossomed trees were forced to flower. They were placed between the marble columns in the large north entry hall through which the guests entered the White House, and again in the East Room where they were entertained after dinner by pianist Rosalyn Tureck playing selections from Bach. The Marine orchestra was playing, and there were those cherry trees with their beautiful blossoms and twinkling lights so that it looked like spring even though it was the end of winter.

Ted Graber, a well-known Los Angeles interior designer who had elegantly redecorated the family residence floors in the White House after the Carters moved out, would often fly to Washington to help supervise the Christmas decorations and the White House Christmas tree, which was always a work of art. Mr. Graber also redid the transition room between the White House residence and the West Wing leading out to the Rose Garden. This room had been dominated by Oriental wallpaper, furniture, and vases, which President Richard Nixon had brought back from China. Mr. Graber, taking advantage of the large panel windows and doors, made the room into an atrium using a garden-green background wallpaper covered with white trillage, ferns, and colorful flowers which gave the room a lighter, fresher feeling.

My White House Medical Office

The first thing I did when I arrived in my White House medical office each morning was to examine the president's tentative schedule for the day. It was prepared by the scheduling office, and put on the desks of his senior aides. The schedule listed the highlights of the president's day, and were handed out to White House correspondents who were free to make it public if they wished. This ceased immediately after the Hinkley shooting so as not to help any future presidential assassins find their targets. President Reagan's schedule for Monday, February 11, 1985, for example, read:

9:30	Fahd briefing.
10:00	Arrival Cere.
	King Fahd of
	Saudi Arabia
2:00	Interview briefing
2:30	Intv. w/NY Times
4:15	Att. Gen. Smith
5:00	Hold (meaning something may be put in)
7:15	State Dinner
	(black tie)

I'd be told days in advance if the president was planning any trips outside the White House, and if the schedule said they were still on,

I'd station myself where he would exit for the motorcade, be it the diplomatic entrance or the Oval Office, and be ready to go with him.

By now I'd start getting telephone reports from members of my staff I had assigned to look after Vice President and Mrs. Bush, the First Lady, or on rare occasions the president if I wasn't able to be with him myself. They'd usually say everything was fine, but now and then they'd want to discuss a medical problem, or suggest ways to improve the care of our distinguished patients. I'd also get the usual run of calls from security people telling me someone taking a public tour of the White House needed medical attention, or from friends visiting Washington who wanted me to give them a guided tour of the president's home.

My White House medical office was really there to serve the president and First Lady, along with the relatively few people who worked in their home such as the ushers, cooks, flower arranger, curator, president's valet, First Lady's maid, and so on. I had a few visits from top presidential advisers such as Attorney General Edwin Meese, who came in with a sore throat, or Chief of Staff Don Regan with an earache. And when the president was about to leave on a trip overseas, I'd ask him and the White House staffers accompanying him to stop by the office so I could give them the immunization injections they needed based on the recommendation of the Centers for Disease Control in Atlanta. I can't remember anyone refusing the shots because it was against their religion, although I had encountered this among my Christian Scientist patients when I was in private practice back in California.

I was also responsible for the medical office and clinic located in the Victorian rococo Old Executive Building a few hundred yards from the White House. I had a staff of doctors and nurses reporting to me, who looked after the on-the-job medical needs of some 2,500 military, Secret Service, communications, and staff people from cleaning people to grounds keepers working in the executive branch.

Foreign dignitaries visiting Washington occasionally had medical problems, which were usually handled by the State Department's medical people. But if they called me, I'd dispatch a doctor from the Walter Reed Army Hospital or Bethesda Naval Medical Center who would examine them as a courtesy and, if necessary, admit them to the hospital for treatment as a guest of the U.S. government.

As I began to settle in, I looked around my suite of offices where I'd be spending most of my time when I was not off traveling with the president. The suite badly needed redecorating, and since the White

House medical unit is funded by the Navy, and since I love ships, I decided on a maritime decor. I brought in some old ship's clocks and other memorabilia, and Dr. Hutton added more from his collection. There was an unattractive model ship in my private office which I replaced with a terrific-looking one borrowed from Dana Wegner, curator of models, for the Naval Research and Development Center in Bethesda.

My office had two huge empty bookcases which gave the place a feeling of inaction. So I asked Curator of White House Artifacts Clement Conger, whose office was just across the hall, if I could borrow some books from among the carloads of new ones regularly sent to the president by their authors and just filed away. I read *California Rich,* a biography of Lord Louis Mountbatten, and a few others. But it was kind of embarrassing because people would keep dropping by the office wanting to borrow books, and I had to say no since they weren't mine. When I left to return home, Mr. Conger insisted I sign a paper saying all the books he'd lent me were present and accounted for.

My medical office was run by my secretary, Gloria Mabe, who had worked for several presidential doctors before me. My office nurse was one of several RNs who rotated every week and looked after White House staffers who came in with minor complaints, gave them shots before going on trips, and was in charge of my medical bag when I was upstairs keeping an eye on the president during some White House event. They wore a portable transceiver with a microphone in their sleeve and an earplug for reception. This enabled them to listen in on the Secret Service band and if someone "went down," they would get a call: "Come up here and don't forget to bring Dr. Smith's bag."

I insisted that all my doctors and nurses be able to handle heart attacks and other emergencies by being trained in ATLS (advanced trauma life support) and ACLS (advanced cardiac life support). Dr. Ruge did not have this requirement, and I received a lot of flack because some of the nurses he hired understood they were there for keeps. They had bought houses, had kids in school, and were planning to stay a while. But if they were unable to complete the emergency training courses they were aced out; I got a lot of tears over it. New nurses who wanted to join my medical staff had to have passed these courses before I'd even consider them.

Chapter Five

The March of Medicine: Washington to Bush

A top tourist attraction in Washington, D.C., is Ford's Theater, where President Abraham Lincoln was assassinated by John Wilkes Booth while sitting in his box watching a popular comedy of the day called *Our American Cousin.*

An annual evening out for today's president is to leave a black-tie reception at the White House and troop over to Ford's Theater for a charity variety show. I attended two of these affairs with President Reagan, who sat in the front row with House Speaker Thomas "Tip" O'Neill and other capital notables, and I'd always look up at Lincoln's flag-draped box and wonder what I'd have done had I been one of the doctors who rushed to his aid after he was shot.

I became interested in how presidential doctors handled their medical responsibilities from the moment I knew I was going to become one myself. What's amazed me the most, of course, are the truly spectacular advances that have been made in the practice of medicine since George Washington was brought into the world on February 22, 1732.

President Washington's medical history is particularly fascinating because, as Dr. J. Worth Estes of the Boston University School of Medicine points out in the January/February 1985 issue of *Medical Heritage,* "it can be reconstructed in more detail than is possible for any other American—or perhaps for anyone anywhere—of his century."

Washington's medical records show that during his lifetime he suffered from what his doctors called "ague (malaria), fever, smallpox, violent pleurisie, severe dysentery, river fever, quinsy (sore throat), rheumatic arm pains, malignant carbuncle (large abscess on his left thigh), influenza, severe pulmonary inflammation (pneumonia), irritation of the right cheek, and finally cynanche trachealis (probably acute epiglottitis), not to mention innumerable dental problems."

We doctors today use specific treatments to get at the root causes of specific diseases. But in Washington's day, to again quote Dr. Estes, "physicians saw disease first as reflecting imbalances in the body's four humors which they identified as blood, phlegm, yellow bile, and black bile. Imbalances among the humors were detected at the bedside as excesses, or deficits, of four corresponding characteristics: heat and cold, moisture and dryness. An excess of heat, for example, implied a fever, while a deficit of heat implied what we still call a 'cold.' "

Colonial doctors used drugs to treat patients just as we do today, although many of them, such as spirits of lavender, cinnamon water, deer antler shavings, sperm whale oil, Venice treacle, and tincture of myrrh, are now little more than medical curiosities. Instead of prescribing drugs to fight specific diseases, doctors back then used them to "fine tune the body's internal balances" (i.e., its "four humors"). They did this, regardless of what they thought had disrupted those balances, by using bleeding, poultices, and purgatives.

Perhaps the most unsettling aspect of Washington's care was his physicians' use of bleeding to "balance" his blood supply by removing "morbid matter." When Washington was on his deathbed, his doctors removed around three quarts of his blood, or nearly half his entire supply, which unquestionably hastened his death and was severely criticized by other physicians at the time. "Very few of the most robust young men in the world could survive such a loss of blood," said Dr. John Brickell of Savannah, Georgia, "but the body of an aged person must be so exhausted, and all his powers so weakened by it as to make his death speedy and inevitable."

In his *Medical Heritage* article, Dr. Estes notes that Washington's first false teeth were made by John Greenwood, his favorite dentist, right before he was inaugurated president in 1789 at age fifty-seven when he had only one tooth left in his lower jaw. Dr. Greenwood's denture consisted of eight human teeth pinned with gold into a plate of elephant or hippopotamus ivory and anchored to his lone remaining tooth. Dr. Greenwood carved another denture out of a walrus tusk a year or so later, and several years after that the artist Charles Wilson Peale crafted a full set of upper and lower dentures out of cow's teeth. Dr. Greenwood continued to make new dentures for Washington right up until a year before his death.

President Grover Cleveland had a far more severe oral cavity problem a century later when he discovered a rough patch on the roof of his mouth which his White House doctor decided might be cancerous and should be removed. The president, along with a team of four physicians and a dentist experienced in administering nitrous oxide, secretly boarded a large private yacht in New York called the *Oneida* whose saloon had been turned into an operating room, according to Stephen Holt Stokes, M.D., writing in the *Journal of the Tennessee Medical Association.*

The medical team was concerned about operating on President Cleveland, who was fifty-six years old in the summer of 1893, quite obese, and visibly tired after his first four months in office, a time dominated by a financial panic caused by the depletion of the nation's gold reserves. It was decided the president's surgery should not be delayed, and as the yacht steamed up the East River at half speed, his medical team extracted President Cleveland's two upper bicuspid teeth, and removed part of his palate and most of his upper jaw—except the orbital plate—in an operation lasting one and a half hours.

President Cleveland's doctors used nitrous oxide to relieve the pain from his surgery, but immediately shifted to ether when it failed to put him to sleep. The president's four doctors and a dentist risked his life, and theirs, by using these two gases in the small operating room they had set up in the yacht's saloon. Nitrous oxide and ether are highly inflammable, and could have been ignited by the yacht's oil lamps, or a spark from the storage battery which powered the instrument used to cauterize, i.e., "heat seal," the bleeding blood vessels in the president's oral cavity and jaw following his operation. "If there's an explosion," commented one of the president's doctors who recognized the danger, "I hope we'll all go down with the ship."

While nitrous oxide and ether are banned from today's surgical suites, they were considered a godsend to medicine in the 1800s. Nitrous oxide, or laughing gas, was used as a carnival attraction before a Boston dentist named Horace Wells began using it in 1846 to do painful teeth extractions. Massachusetts General Hospital soon began administering nitrous oxide to reduce pain during general surgery, followed soon after by its acceptance as a general anesthesia. Ether was used for years even though it was slow in putting patients to sleep, slow in allowing them to wake up, and frequently responsible for induced coughing, nausea, vomiting, and other disagreeable reactions.

President Cleveland quickly recovered from his operation, arriving at his Gray Gables presidential retreat four days after surgery. Two weeks later, however, his doctor detected a suspicious area near his wound, and the president once again boarded the *Oneida* for additional surgery, returning to Gray Gables the next day. His wound had been packed with gauze, and although his speech was labored he could be clearly understood. When the gauze was removed, however, he was unintelligible. Dr. K. Gibson, a prosthodontist, set up a dental laboratory at Gray Gables and fashioned a vulcanized rubber prosthesis which allowed Mr. Cleveland to speak normally again. The president had no further trouble with his oral cancer, ultimately dying of coronary artery disease fifteen years later.

Dentist friends of mine tell me that President Cleveland received state-of-the-art care back in 1893, and that all modern dentistry could do to improve upon it would be to replace the vulcanized rubber prosthesis with a similar one made of acrylic plastic.

There was a question, however, as to whether President Cleveland actually had an oral cancer requiring surgical removal and replacement by prosthesis. The original biopsy report done by a Dr. Welch of Johns Hopkins University prior to the surgery was never found. Follow-up studies of the actual tissue removed from the mass on the roof of the president's mouth indicate it was probably a verrucous carcinoma. This is a very low grade, benign type of tumor which does not spread to other parts of the body and can usually be excised quite easily. The fact that President Cleveland lived for fifteen more years without any recurrence of the problem suggests this was indeed the case.

Great advances took place in the practice of medicine during the second half of the nineteenth century. The advent of anesthesia in particular made possible painless and prolonged surgery on patients, even though a majority of them died from postoperative infections which were particularly common among wounded soldiers during the Civil War.

This type of "contact infection" was first identified in 1846 by a Hungarian physician named Ignaz Semmelweis while he was working in the Obstetrical Clinic in Vienna. Dr. Semmelweis found that simply washing his hands between patients reduced the alarming rate of deaths from "childbed fever" following the normal deliveries of babies.

Dr. Joseph Lister in Scotland was the first to reduce "contact infection" by using carbolic acid to clean his hands and instruments, as well as dressing his patients' wounds, in order to reduce the possibility of infection. Dr. Lister was ridiculed and discredited by the medical profession until 1880 when Robert Koch in Germany identified bacteria as the cause of infection.

All of these medical breakthroughs originated in Europe and were slow to be embraced by the American medical profession. This can be seen in the uninformed way physicians treated infection during their valiant efforts to save the lives of Presidents James A. Garfield and William McKinley after they were shot by a disgruntled office seeker and an anarchist, respectively.

It was not uncommon for presidents to keep their illnesses private. Grover Cleveland attempted to keep his infirmities from the prying eyes of the press, as did Woodrow Wilson, who suffered two strokes that turned him into a virtual invalid during the last eighteen months of his presidency; Franklin D. Roosevelt, whose already paralyzed body was ravaged by heart failure and hypertension from 1943 until his death on April 12, 1945; and John F. Kennedy, whose vitality was compromised by adrenal deficiency and chronic back pain throughout his thousand days in the White House.

The practice of medicine has made amazing strides in recent years, and I've often wondered whether modern techniques could have saved the lives of Abraham Lincoln, James A. Garfield, William McKinley, and John F. Kennedy, who were all assassinated while in office, just as it saved Ronald Reagan following the near-fatal attempt on his life in 1981.

I'm certain that nothing medicine has today could have saved Abraham Lincoln, or John Kennedy.

President Lincoln was killed by John Wilkes Booth, a twenty-six-year-old actor who had quietly entered the presidential box a few minutes after 10 P.M. on April 14, 1865, held a single-shot Derringer pistol an inch from the back of Mr. Lincoln's head, and fired. The bullet went through the president's brain and lodged behind his left eye, according to *Abraham Lincoln: A History,* written by two close associates who were with him when he died at 7:22 A.M. the following morning having never regained consciousness.

There is a small museum directly beneath Ford's Theater filled with memorabilia of the tragedy, from the clothes Lincoln wore to the blood-stained pillow which cradled his head, to Booth's small pistol which ended Lincoln's life at age fifty-six. Dr. Charles A. Leale, a young Army doctor who reached President Lincoln minutes after he was shot, managed to restore his breathing even though he knew he would die. "His wound," said Dr. Leale, "is mortal. It is impossible for him to recover."

The high-powered bullets Lee Harvey Oswald fired at President John F. Kennedy's open limousine from the sixth floor of the Dallas

Book Depository Building were even more deadly than the lone shot which killed Lincoln, since they pierced the base of JFK's neck, while his right arm was raised waving to the crowds, and opened a massive, gaping wound on the right side of his head. President Kennedy, according to an article in the January 1964 issue of the *Texas State Journal of Medicine,* was moribund when he arrived at Parkland Memorial Hospital's Trauma Room One shortly after 12:30 P.M. on November 22, 1963, and was pronounced dead at 1 P.M. by Dr. William Kemp Clark.

Controversy has continued to swirl about the cause of death of President Kennedy. Demands to reopen an investigation have been forthcoming and the recent film *JFK* has created distrust in the investigations that were conducted years ago.

The May 27, 1992, issue of the *Journal of the American Medical Association* carries an interview of the two Navy pathologists who performed the autopsy on President Kennedy the evening of his death. They have not broken their silence since that night of November 22, 1963. Drs. Boswell and Hume feel their findings are conclusive that the fatal wounds were the result of two bullets that came from above and behind. They further assert that there was no interference from the military or the FBI and that the examination was straightforward.

A companion article recalls the memories of the four Parkland Hospital physicians who tried unsuccessfully to sustain the life of President John F. Kennedy. Their recall should end the conspiracy theories but it is likely that people will not change.

While modern medicine could not have helped Lincoln and Kennedy, it could certainly have saved the life of President James A. Garfield, if contemporary accounts of the shooting are accurate. I think the case could be made, as a matter of fact, that the best medicine of the time could also have saved him had it been used more expeditiously.

President Garfield was shot in Washington's Baltimore and Potomac Railroad station on July 2, 1881, as he was leaving on a trip to show his two sons around his old alma mater, Williams College in Massachusetts, which they would be entering in the fall. The president's only guard was a Washington, D.C., policeman, and as he walked toward his train he was attacked by Charles J. Guiteau, an unbalanced lawyer and evangelist who had been denied a government job. Guiteau fired two shots at President Garfield from his English bulldog .44-caliber revolver, one shot grazing Mr. Garfield's sleeve, the other hitting him in the back near the spine.

Theodore Clarke Smith, professor of American history at Williams College, describes the assassination of President Garfield in his book *The Life and Letters of James Abram Garfield.* Dr. Alfred Jay Bollet, clinical professor of medicine at Yale's Medical School, wrote a detailed article on it in the July 1981 issue of *Medical Times* likening the shooting to the attempt on President Reagan's life one hundred years later.

After President Garfield was shot, he slumped to the ground and was carried to the second floor of the station, where his old boyhood friend Dr. D. W. Bliss gave him half an ounce of brandy, a dram of spirits of ammonia, and began searching for the bullet with his little finger and a long silver probe similar to the one used to investigate President Lincoln's wound sixteen years earlier.

Garfield was taken to the White House in a horse-drawn ambulance, and from the symptoms it was agreed that he was hemorrhaging internally and could not survive the night. Vice President Chester A. Arthur was told to get ready to take the oath of office. But the president rallied, felt much better the next morning, and asked Dr. Bliss to put a medical team together to look after him, which he did, picking two Army surgeons and three civilian doctors from Washington, Philadelphia, and New York.

The six doctors decided that none of the president's internal organs had been hurt, but agreed to keep a sharp eye out for signs of infection. The president was moved to a corner room in the White House cooled by air piped in from the basement after a fan had drawn it through 3,000 feet of toweling dripping with salted ice water. By July 13, Garfield's doctors were able to announce that the president's "gradual progress toward complete recovery is manifest and thus far without serious complications."

But on July 23, Garfield developed a chill and his temperature shot up to 104 degrees. His doctors traced the problem to pus found in the channel the surgeons had created with their probes; it was cut open and cleaned out. This gave the president relief, and the daily bulletins were again hopeful until August 18, when a swelling appeared in the parotid gland in his neck, which began discharging pus through his mouth and ear. By August 26, the president's doctors felt the situation was practically hopeless. Members of the cabinet were told that death was near, Vice President Arthur was again notified to stand by, and the Washington press corps ran reports saying the president's condition was hopeless.

But again President Garfield rallied, and on September 6 he was moved by special train from his sickroom in the White House to a cottage by the sea in Elberon, New Jersey, overlooking the Atlantic Ocean (more than 2,000 volunteers had spent the prior day building a 3,200-foot track from the railroad's main line to the front door of the house). President Garfield seemed to improve, and by September 8 three of his six doctors had retired from his case. On September 13 he was sitting up and watching the ocean. "This is delightful," he was reported as saying, "I am myself again."

His apparent recovery ended on September 17 when his fever increased, his pulse fluttered, and he partially lost consciousness. His terribly emaciated body made the situation almost hopeless, and everyone around him knew the end was near. On the night of September 19, Dr. Bliss was called for, and as Mrs. Garfield held her husband's hand, he examined his patient. "Applying my ear over the heart," Dr. Bliss said, "I detected an indistinct fluttering which continued until 10:35 when he expired."

The medical profession has changed almost beyond recognition in the just over a century since America's twentieth president was killed by an assassin's bullet.

In those days, doctors used to probe for bullets with their fingers, with instruments, and with other nonsterile techniques, feeling that if a bullet were removed, everything would be fine. Today we know the bullet was never the problem because a hot bullet is self-sterilizing. The real problem was all the ill-advised, ill-directed probing that was done repeatedly by every doctor who entered President Garfield's sickroom and thought he could do a better job than the one before. All that probing introduced more, and probably different types of bacteria along the path of the bullet as it tunneled through Garfield's body, eventually killing America's twentieth president.

It's interesting to note, by the way, that at the trial of Charles Guiteau, who shot Garfield and was later hanged, the defense argued that it wasn't their client who killed the president, but rather his doctors. They were probably right.

If President Garfield had been shot in the back today, we'd put a sterile dressing over his wound, make sure nobody touched it, and immediately administer antibiotics to treat any infectious bacteria which had been carried into the wound by bits of fabric from his clothes or debris from the bullet itself. We'd then hustle him into his armored limousine which would have been waiting outside the railroad station, and the presidential motorcade would have then dashed for the nearest predetermined hospital just as the Secret Service ordered it to do after President Reagan was shot.

Once inside the hospital's emergency room we'd check the president's appearance, pulse, and blood pressure, and start putting blood and other fluids back into his body intravenously to reduce shock. We'd monitor his heart with an electrocardiogram. We'd give him a broad-spectrum antibiotic to prevent the onset of infection. We'd do a red blood count to see if he was still losing blood and a white blood count to monitor if any infection was developing which would be treated with appropriate antibiotics. We'd use an X ray or computerized axial tomography (CAT) scan to locate the bullet, which we might decide to leave alone because it might mean a second anesthesia and surgical procedure which could create more problems than the bullet itself.

President Garfield's doctors never found the bullet that killed him, even though others were fired into cadavers in an effort to reproduce the wound. Alexander Graham Bell was also asked to search for the bullet using an apparatus hooked up to his recently invented telephone, which was said to emit a hum when passed over a piece of metal, much like today's metal detectors. When the bullet was eventually located during an autopsy on Garfield's body, it was found in his back muscle, a far less dangerous place than his physicians had thought.

We modern doctors would then monitor President Garfield to see if there was any intestinal damage by doing what's called a four-quadrant tap. A hollow needle would be inserted in four different places in his abdomen to see if we obtained air, blood, intestinal contents, or nothing indicating whether the bullet had perforated the bowel, gone through the intestines, cut the liver, and so on. If we wanted to get still more information, we could do an X ray, CAT scan, magnetic resonance imaging examination, or even exploratory surgery to see if all the organs were intact.

If President Garfield had received this quality of medical care he would have had no problems, and in four or five weeks would have been back at work. He certainly wouldn't have died of septicemia produced by deadly bacteria entering the bloodstream.

President William McKinley's injury was more serious than President Garfield's, but I believe he too could have been saved by modern medicine judging by an eyewitness account of the shooting by Buffalo *Enquirer* writer Richard Barry, published in *America: Great Crises in*

Our History Told by Its Makers, and Margaret Leech's monumental biography *In the Days of McKinley*.

President McKinley was assassinated on Friday, September 6, 1901, while greeting children prior to giving a speech in the Temple of Music of the Pan-American Exposition in Buffalo, New York. The floor in front of the podium in the nearly empty hall was packed with wooden folding chairs, and the fifty-eight-year-old president was well guarded by exposition police, Buffalo city detectives, U.S. artillery men, and three Secret Service agents.

Thousands of people were crowded in front of the doors waiting to enter the hall on this steamy hot day, and when the president said, "Let them come," they surged in, filling the huge room within minutes. Caught up in the stampede was a slim, twenty-eight-year-old anarchist named Leon F. Czolgosz, dressed in a dark woolen suit, flannel shirt, and string tie, who he held a .32-caliber Iver-Johnson revolver in his right hand wrapped in a dirty handkerchief. A detective standing nearby saw Czolgosz and remarked, "This man has a sore hand."

Another detective wasn't so sure, and as he reached for Czolgosz's gun hand the assassin fired two shots, hitting President McKinley in the chest and abdomen. Czolgosz was immediately subdued by a dozen men, one of whom smashed his nose, as the president, still standing, was helped to a nearby bench by his secretary George Cortelyou and the president of the exposition, John Milburn.

An ambulance arrived within minutes, and the president, now bathed in blood, was taken to the exposition's emergency hospital, which was scarcely more than a first-aid station, and laid on a table in a state of severe shock. One of the shots Czolgosz fired at him had merely grazed his ribs, but the other one had opened up a serious abdominal wound. Dr. Mathew D. Mann, a prominent Buffalo surgeon, was summoned, and he and three assistant surgeons decided to operate immediately even though the afternoon light in the small room was failing and the electric lighting was inadequate. One of the doctors attempted to compensate by using a hand mirror to reflect the rays of the setting sun through the president's incision and into the abdominal cavity. Toward the end of the operation, the doctors did manage to rig up an electric light.

When the surgeons opened the president's abdomen, they found the bullet had perforated the front and back wall of his stomach. Thus, they sutured the tears and cleaned out the peritoneal cavity as best as they could. Again the bullet was not found, even though one of the first X-ray machines was on display nearby at the exposition and offered to McKinley's physicians. The president's incision was eventually closed without drainage and covered with an antiseptic dressing.

President McKinley was carried unconscious to exposition President John Milburn's home, and put in a bedroom on the second floor which was turned into a hospital. Vice President Theodore Roosevelt rushed to the president's bedside by special train, and for the next few days hopes for a complete recovery were so high that Roosevelt felt he could rejoin his family on holiday in the Adirondack Mountains, even though the house they were staying in was forty-two miles from the nearest telegraph wire.

On Thursday morning, September 12, President McKinley felt so well that he had a breakfast of toast, coffee, beef juice, and chicken broth topped off with a cigar. The weather was perfect, and it was felt the president would soon be his old self. But that evening he took a turn for the worse, and his physicians gave him violent purgatives to cleanse his system. At 2:30 A.M. on Friday, President McKinley suffered a physical collapse, his pulse, in the words of newspaperman Richard Barry, "had ceased its throb," and official bulletins said little more than "hope against hope."

That morning, however, President McKinley's pulse and temperature returned to normal. Later that day, after passing through the sentries surrounding the Milburn home, the president's secretary George Cortelyou paid his regular visit to the more than one hundred newspaper reporters crowded into the press tent across the street, and told them, "If the president lives until morning there will be grounds for hope."

It wasn't long after Cortelyou's trip to the press tent that President McKinley lapsed into unconsciousness. A heart specialist from Washington had sped to the president's bedside by electric automobile and arrived at midnight. But he was too late, and at 2:15 A.M. on Saturday morning, September 14, 1901, President McKinley died. His last words were, "Good-bye all, good-bye. It is God's will. His will, not ours, be done."

Modern surgery would treat a gunshot wound, like the one which took President McKinley's life, in a methodical manner with careful attention to the perforation of the stomach and intestinal tract. These tears would be sutured to prevent infection from the contents of his stomach and intestines which may have spilled out into his body, or from bits of clothing and other debris which may have been introduced into it by the bullet. What's worrisome is the possibility of digestive juices leaking from the pancreas into the abdominal cavity. This may have been responsible for McKinley's death, and to help control it, we'd insert a sterile drain into the abdominal cavity so that any pancreatic fluid, blood, or infectious material would be drained away until healing was complete.

As McKinley was recovering from his operation, we'd use intravenous fluids to make sure he was adequately hydrated, and correct any imbalance in his electrolytes, including potassium. Since no real cause of McKinley's death was found during a careful autopsy, I believe he probably died from a low potassium level. We know he lost potassium through repeated enemas and laxatives, and since physicians back then were unaware of the need to replace this key body chemical, it seems likely that it killed him.

Advances in Presidential Security

Although President McKinley was assassinated in this century, the protection he received before he was shot, and the care he was given afterward were positively primitive by modern medical standards.

If President George Bush were scheduled to visit a Pan-American exposition in Buffalo today it would be "preadvanced" weeks ahead of time by experts responsible for (1) getting him to and from the event; (2) ensuring his security; (3) making certain he could communicate with anyone in the world he needed to reach; and (4) arranging for the best possible medical care should he be injured or taken ill.

Medical planning begins the moment a presidential trip is scheduled. The White House physician must know what medical personnel will be needed, where immediate assessment and stabilization can be carried out if needed, and whether the president should be treated immediately or later either by ambulance paramedics enroute to a definitive care hospital or at the hospital itself.

This last decision is usually made in terms of "scoop and run" versus "on the spot." In the first instance the president would be scooped up and rushed to the nearest definitive care hospital, where his injury would be assessed and his condition stabilized. In the second he'd receive intravenous fluids at the place of injury, bleeding would be stopped, blood pressure taken, wounds dressed, fractures splinted or neck braces applied, and a supply of oxygen ensured.

If shots rang out, the Secret Service detail guarding the president would surround him, all exits from the building would be barred to prevent the shooter from escaping, and the White House doctor and two nurses would be at the president's side before he fell to the floor. The standby ambulance staffed with paramedics would be summoned, and the waiting motorcade alerted along with the emergency room of the nearest designated hospital.

One of the nurses would begin evaluating the president's heart rate and blood pressure, while checking to make sure his breathing was unobstructed. The other nurse would insert a needle into one of the president's veins to start fluids flowing into his body, and the doctor would assess the extent of his injuries and then alert the hospital emergency room to get ready to receive him. All this would take about forty-five seconds.

The monitoring of the president's condition would continue as he was carried into the ambulance, where electrocardiogram leads would be attached to his chest and the results transmitted directly to the hospital's emergency room along with other pertinent information on his condition. The hospital could use these data in assembling a medical team which would be ready to swing into action the moment the president arrived, and in deciding whether the X-ray room, blood bank, laboratory, and surgical suite should be told to stand by.

Armed Secret Service agents would continue doing everything possible to protect the president while enroute to the hospital and during his stay there. The president's press secretary would be struggling to keep literally screaming reporters informed of his condition. The military would be put on alert in case the shooting was part of a conspiracy to overthrow the government. Vice President Dan Quayle would have been located and told to stay in a safe place should it be necessary to invoke the Twenty-fifth Amendment to the Constitution and install him as temporary president of the United States.

President Bush would now be in a definitive care hospital, and if he was not moribund, as President Kennedy was when he arrived at Parkland Memorial Hospital in Dallas, he would be taken to X-ray in an effort to locate the bullet (or bullets) and to assess the damage to the bony structure of his body. If the president's condition was stable, and if he was not in shock, a conference would be held among the physicians treating him to decide on the optimum surgical procedure.

The doctors' decision would be reviewed with President Bush and the First Lady, and the transfer of presidential power to Vice President Quayle would be discussed and carried out if necessary. Members of the president's cabinet would gather in the White House to assist "President" Quayle in governing the nation. And the State Department would notify foreign embassies of the situation so they could inform their governments.

I spent two years as the White House physician to Ronald Reagan and George Bush and have tremendous empathy for the doctors who were responsible for the lives of Presidents Garfield and McKinley because I've been there and know what happens after a shooting. There are confusion, panic, hysteria, and lack of leadership. There is the awesome burden that suddenly falls on the head surgeon, who must decide what kind of surgery to perform, where to do it, and when to do it. Additionally, there is an unending barrage of questions from the reporters insisting on the public's "right to know" since it's the president of the United States lying there on the operating table. And then there's the outpouring of second-guessing and criticism, which always follow regardless of the outcome.

This is the train of events which takes on a life of its own from the moment the bullet leaves an assassin's gun. And it can happen today as we saw when President Reagan was shot at close range by John Hinkley, Jr., outside the Washington Hilton Hotel.

The practice of medicine has changed virtually beyond recognition in the years since McKinley's death as I was reminded when I received an unpublished manuscript from the son of Dr. Howard Snyder, who was White House physician to President Dwight D. Eisenhower. In the manuscript, Dr. Snyder gives a detailed account of how he cared for Ike following his massive and near fatal heart attack on September 24, 1955, when he and his wife, Mamie, were staying at her mother's home in Denver.

Mrs. Eisenhower called Dr. Snyder at 2:54 A.M. on September 25, according to his manuscript, to say the sixty-four-year-old president "had pain in his lower chest and upper abdomen and that she had given him milk of magnesia without relief." Dr. Snyder was staying at the nearby Lowry Air Force Base and covered the six miles to the president's side in seventeen minutes, arriving at 3:11 A.M.

Dr. Snyder said he found the president "was agitated and complaining of severe pain across his chest." He gave the president an intramuscular injection of papaverine hydrochloride, a sniff of amyl nitrite to help dilate his blood vessels, morphine to relieve the pain, and heparin to prevent blood clotting. Dr. Snyder tried to give oxygen to President Eisenhower, but he would not tolerate the mask. Sergeant Moaney, Ike's favorite orderly, rubbed him with warm alcohol and piled hot water bottles around his body. Despite this treatment, President Eisenhower "went into a state of shock. His blood pressure collapsed, and his pulse rate climbed alarmingly and again became quite irregular."

At 4:05 A.M., Dr. Snyder said he asked Mamie "to slip into bed and wrap herself around the president to see if this would quiet him and assist in warming his body. This had the desired effect almost immediately. The president settled down and went to sleep quietly. Mamie remained in bed with him until about 6 A.M., when she, without disturbing him, returned to her own bed."

President Eisenhower slept until 11:30 A.M., and shortly thereafter Dr. Snyder asked the top cardiologist from the nearby Fitzsimons Army Hospital to come out and examine the president. He arrived at 1 P.M., and after talking with Dr. Snyder, examining the president, and taking an electrocardiogram, he told Dr. Snyder that the president had suffered a massive heart attack. At 1:30 P.M., Dr. Snyder had two husky men carry the president downstairs. Then, in order not to alarm members of the press gathered outside the house, Dr. Snyder had President Eisenhower walk to his waiting limousine and sit in the back seat for the short drive to the VIP suite at Fitzsimons, where he continued his recovery until he returned to the White House on November 11.

President Eisenhower certainly could have died. But Dr. Snyder gave him an opiate to relieve the pain, and did everything medically that was known at the time, which undoubtedly saved President Eisenhower's life.

It's interesting to note that in 1955, just thirty-seven years ago, there was little to be gained from moving President Eisenhower, or any other heart attack patient to a hospital since bed rest was the treatment of choice back then.

There were no coronary care units to continuously monitor patients' condition, no medication to break up a clot which might appear in the coronary vessels supplying the heart with blood, or prevent a new clot from forming. Angiograms, or X-ray pictures of the heart, were not available to help diagnose blocked blood vessels which could trigger a heart attack. Blood tests to follow heart damage were not in use. Defibrillators to reverse the life-threatening uncoordinated beating of the heart hadn't been invented. Open-heart cardiac massage was not in general use. And we hadn't yet learned how to track the heart's rate and rhythm from one second to the next. Just about the only thing a doctor had to gain from moving a heart attack patient to a hospital was shared responsibility for the patient's care.

If Eisenhower were president today and had a heart attack in his mother-in-law's home, I'd pop an aspirin down him right away, give him an injection of the latest thrombolytic agents to lessen the chance of a blood clot, and hook him up to an electrocardiograph machine the size of a large briefcase I carried with me everywhere I went. This machine would monitor the rhythm of his heart and automatically shock it back to a normal beat if it began to fibrillate wildly.

I'd then get him to the coronary care unit of a nearby hospital as fast as possible where I'd supersaturate his bloodstream with oxygen because his heart would be crying out for it. This treatment, reflecting what we've learned about handling massive heart attacks in the nearly thirty-five years since President Eisenhower was stricken, would have further increased his chances for survival and significantly reduced the seven weeks or so it took before he was ready to return to work.

The medical care surrounding the president of the United States today is so advanced it's difficult to think of ways it might be improved.

The White House medical unit is superbly organized, equipped, and staffed as demonstrated when President Bush's doctors allowed him to return to the Oval Office less than forty-eight hours after the onset of his erratic heartbeat on Saturday, May 4, 1991.

The president's heart flutter happened while he was spending the weekend at Camp David, and was out for his Saturday morning jog surrounded by a group of Secret Service agents. The most popular jogging trail at Camp David is the perimeter road, which runs around the place just inside its double security fence. The trail goes through some hilly terrain, but is not too challenging and is a favorite of the military and Secret Service people assigned to protect the president, who usually completes this run with ease.

But on this occasion, the president suddenly developed a shortness of breath, and became quite weak, which was unusual for him. The Secret Service probably checked his pulse which would have been irregular, and advised him to stop by Camp David's sick bay, i.e., infirmary. Although I wasn't there, I've spent enough time at Camp David to know that the president's doctor was immediately alerted by walkie-talkie radio, and was by his side within minutes. The doctor undoubtedly took his blood pressure, had him lie down, hooked him up to an electrocardiograph machine, and may have started giving him oxygen, along with intravenous fluids in a vein in his arm in case he had to have emergency medications. All this would have happened within a few minutes during which the White House Secret Service command post and the president's chief of staff would have been notified, and the presidential helicopter and crew alerted that Mr. Bush might have to be flown out of Camp David at a moment's notice.

The president's heart was the overriding concern since the electrocardiogram no doubt showed an irregular and rapid beat of the atrium, and a normal, but slow ventricular rate. The questions uppermost in the mind of President Bush's doctor, of course, were what had caused the irregularity in his heartbeat and what might happen next? Could it be advance warning of an impending heart attack, or might the president's entire heart begin to fibrillate wildly, leading to almost certain death unless it could be stopped?

Here was the president of the United States with what could be a very serious heart problem, and the nearest coronary care unit was in a civilian hospital in Hagerstown, Maryland, some seven and a half air miles away (the Naval Hospital in Bethesda where presidents are usually treated was worse at twenty-five air miles away). An electronic tracing of the president's heartbeat could have been sent by telephone to the heart unit at Bethesda, and a simultaneous consultation held. But whatever the decision, President Bush would be flown to Bethesda for monitoring, to try and prevent any lethal changes which might take place, and to do everything medically possible to correct his abnormal heart activity.

Continued observation and testing of President Bush's physical condition soon indicated that his heart rate had returned to normal following the use of irritation-reducing medications. He was also given a drug called Coumadin to prevent blood clots from forming in the atrium of the heart that might suddenly pass to the brain producing a strokelike situation. These initial medications proved effective, and the president was allowed to resume his normal workload.

Further tests on the president, however, disclosed that an overactive thyroid was the reason for the irritation of his heart. This was something which could be corrected by treating the thyroid gland with radioactive material which will ultimately destroy the gland's secretion of a hormone necessary for active bodily function. This therapy has been used for forty years, and so far there have been no known side effects. Fortunately, the amount of thyroid hormone necessary for active bodily function can be artificially substituted by taking thyroid hormone medication for life.

It was four months before a long-term evaluation of the president's heart problem could be conducted by subjecting him to a number of cardiac appraisals, including a stress test on a treadmill. These tests convinced the president's doctors that they could stop his heart medications, and that he could resume the consumption of alcohol and other stimulants in moderation, and immediately get back to vigorous physical activities such as jogging or hiking in the Grand Canyon. President Bush's doctors also saw no medical reason why he could not run for a second term in the White House in 1992.

The heart flutter President Bush experienced while jogging at Camp David has been brought under control by his physicians using the best modern medicine has to offer. About the only other medical advance I can think of which might prove useful would be to permanently implant a small electronic device in his body which would allow White House doctors to continually monitor his heart. This idea is not so far-fetched. A few days after President Bush experienced erratic heart rhythm, his doctors had him wear a device around his waist which transmitted a continuous electrocardiogram they could read while he went about his normal activities.

Chapter Six

A Picture of Health

My medical office in the basement of the White House was directly opposite the elevator serving the Reagans' family quarters located on the second and third floors of the White House. There was a desk in front of the elevator manned by a member of the Secret Service which guards the president, and a uniformed member of the Presidential Protective Detail which guards the White House. The president used to come down in the elevator every morning at 9 A.M., his arrival heralded by a chorus of ringing bells, and the frantic barking and rushing about of his sheepdog Lucky, who jumped up and greeted him the instant he appeared.

Jim Kuhn was always there waiting for him. And I'd stand outside my office door in case he wanted to chat, or I wanted to suggest he stop by on his way home for immunization shots he might need for an upcoming trip. I didn't know how his schedule would run that day, or what emergencies he'd have to deal with, but I wanted him to know I'd be waiting to give him his injection "if it's convenient." When the time finally came for him and the First Lady to get their immunization injections, I'd always use vaccines from new, unopened bottles that couldn't have been tampered with. If there was any vaccine left, I'd use it on myself and other White House people accompanying him on the trip.

Most of the time the president would simply wave and say good morning as he strode past my office, through the White House basement, out into the colonnade bordering the Rose Garden, and into the Oval Office in the West Wing, which President Theodore Roosevelt had built in 1902 to separate where he worked from where he lived. President Reagan enjoyed feeding acorns, which he had gathered for them the weekend before at Camp David, to the squirrels scampering around outside the Oval Office. The squirrels' playground had once been the site of a putting green installed by President Eisenhower but was later removed by President Nixon, who felt it was too difficult to maintain.

This walk to work gave me my first chance of the day to observe President Reagan, who always looked perfect. He was smiling, animated, impeccably groomed, and in good humor, with a neat bundle of papers he had worked on the night before in his hand. I'd keep an eye on him throughout the day in case he suddenly became pale, weak, or clammy, slurred his words, or stumbled. I was ready to rush to his side and take over no matter where he was or what he was doing.

I also looked for signs of aging in the president. Yet I never detected a tremor as he raised a glass to his lips, a lack of interest when doing something such as saddling his horse at his ranch, a wobble in his signature, simple forgetfulness, screwing up when telling a joke or story, or a change in his grip when shaking hands. Sometimes we'd have a little chat in the morning, and I wouldn't see him again until the end of the day when he'd pick right up on our conversation as if nothing had happened. I thought that too was a pretty good check on his well-being, particularly because he was always as upbeat at the end of an arduous day as he was at the beginning. I've often wondered if President Reagan used his training as an actor to make himself appear better on the outside than he was actually feeling on the inside. The First Lady was different. I've seen her quite obviously distressed and upset, and I've seen her laughing uproariously, making no effort I could detect to hide her true inner feelings.

The president has a strong handshake. When he waves with his left hand, however, it is possible to detect a minor ailment which made it impossible for him to straighten the ring finger on his left hand. It is a condition called Dupuytren's contracture, named after Baron Guillaume Dupuytren, a French surgeon who discussed its cause and correction back in 1831. The condition is fairly common among men over fifty, particularly if they're of Celtic or northern European descent like the president, and it tends to get worse over the years until, in some cases, the bent finger appears glued to the palm of the hand.

The president's finger hadn't reached this point, but it was awkward, and on January 7, 1989, Dr. John Hutton, who replaced me as physician to the president, led the three-man team of orthopedic and plastic surgeons who operated on President Reagan at Walter Reed Army Medical Center to correct the condition. The president was given a local anesthesia which allowed him to chat with his doctors, and tell a few stories during the operation which took just over three hours. When it was over, the bend in his ring finger was gone. President Reagan told me recently at the Los Angeles Country Club that he can now grip a golf club with no difficulty.

Whenever the president gave a speech at some function or other, we'd all go into a holding room where we'd stay for a few minutes until they were ready for him to make his entrance. This room, like virtually everyplace else the president visited when away from the White House, had been previously debugged and secured by the Secret Service, and equipped with a scrambler telephone plugged directly into the White House switchboard by the White House Communications Agency, familiarly known as WHCA (pronounced "wa-ca").

One time we were waiting in a holding room in a school in Virginia where the president was to give a speech, when White House Chief of Staff Don Regan grabbed me and said the boss's eye was bloodshot. I went over to where the president was standing studying his notes, and saw he had a subconjunctival hemorrhage, or burst blood vessel, which is an extremely common problem that lasts for about eight to ten days and can be caused by anything from hypertension to sneezing. It doesn't hurt, and most people aren't even aware anything's wrong. But it's scary to look at someone and see a blood-red eye staring back at you. We told the president what had happened and he said, "I've had them before," and continued to read his notes.

Ronald Reagan loves to tell stories, and can retrieve one from memory to fit almost any occasion, including how hazardous it is to tell a story when you're not sure who's in the audience.

One of his favorites is about the last survivor of the great Johnstown Flood, who eventually died and was welcomed at the Pearly Gates by St. Peter himself. "It's wonderful to have a great celebrity like you here in heaven," said St. Peter. "My pleasure," said the man, "would you like me to give a speech about how to survive a flood?" "Sounds good," said St. Peter, "but don't overdo it because there's an old fellow out in the audience named Noah."

Then there's the golf story President Reagan told on jaunts around the country as he urged his fellow Republicans to work harder in an unsuccessful campaign to elect GOP congressional candidates in 1986: A father took his son out into a field to teach him about golf. The father tees the golf ball up near an anthill, and tells his son to hit the ball with his driver. The youngster swings, misses the ball, and hits an anthill. Then he tees up again, takes another mighty swing, and demolishes another anthill. At this point one terrified ant turns to the other and says, "If we hope to get out of here alive we better get on the ball."

People loved Ronald Reagan, and when he was the guest speaker at some function or other they'd pay almost anything just to shake his hand. They tended to get carried away. They'd see the president standing there, and for a contribution of only a few thousand dollars to the Republican party, a charity, or whatever, they could actually shake his hand, say hi, and get a picture taken with him which they'd treasure for the rest of their lives.

I'll never forget this one scene where everybody was lined up to pay $1,000 apiece to have their picture taken with the president one after the other. One gal was dying to get a picture, but her husband kept saying, "No, I'm not going to do it." But she finally prevails, he pulls out his checkbook, she bends over, he writes his check out on her back, they get into line, hand the check to somebody, get their picture snapped with the president, and leave.

VVIPs (Very Very Important People) were also eager to meet Ronald Reagan, and one person who said he could arrange it was Carl R. Channell, a conservative fund-raiser who produced millions for the Nicaraguan contras. He'd tell these multimillionaires that for $50,000 he could get them in to see the president, and they'd pay up. He didn't promise them a visit with the president, just a chance to see him and get a picture, and since he couldn't always deliver on this promise it got him into a lot of trouble.

Ronald Reagan is such a soft sell he can't say no to this kind of adulation, which played havoc with his incredibly tight schedule. After talks to groups of influential supporters, a rope line would often be set up so the president could walk along shaking hands and saying hello to well-wishers standing on the other side. Once he started doing this, we'd almost have to pull him away because he hated to leave. What really chilled me was when he was about two-thirds of the way down the line and someone took out a pen and asked for his autograph. If just one individual did this, everybody who had already shaken his hand would get back in line to get one too. The president loved this, and he'd do it all day long even though Air Force One was revving up and his motorcade was ready to roll. Finally, Jim Kuhn or someone else would have to break in and say, "Mr. President, we've got to go."

One time my sister and brother-in-law, Frances and Dana Leavitt, were in town, and I took the night off so Kit and I could go out to dinner with them (after assigning Dr. Savage to be with the president).

I had made arrangements through Jim Kuhn for the four of us to be lined up to have our picture taken with the president when he returned to the White House after a speaking engagement in Washington at 9 P.M. As we were driving back from the restaurant, I heard the sound of the "Nighthawk" helicopter which always flies above the president's motorcade peering down on the tops of buildings. I looked at my watch and it was twenty minutes before nine, yet the president was obviously on his way home. So we rushed to get back, but the president had already arrived and was upstairs in his quarters. I told everybody it was too bad, but the president had finished early and we were out of luck.

As we were preparing to leave, Dr. Savage spotted me and said, "Where were you? The president is looking forward to meeting your family." Then a Secret Service agent arrived and said, "Hey, Jim Kuhn is looking for you." When Jim saw us he said, "Look, stand here at the bottom of the elevator. The president is looking for you, and he wants his picture." I said, "Where is he?" Jim said, "He's up in the residence." I said, "Well, I'm not going to make him come back downstairs; you just don't do that." "But he wants to do it," Jim said. So, by golly, down he came in the elevator. I felt terrible because, you know, you don't do this to the president of the United States of America. But he must have remembered that members of my family were visiting me, so down he came. We all lined up so White House photographer Bill Fitzpatrick could take the picture. The president shook hands with everybody and went back upstairs.

Presidential "photo opportunities" like the one we had take only a few seconds, but seem like an eternity because people are so awed by finding themselves standing next to the president.

The White House has several photographers who record every event. I noticed that many of them used Nikon cameras, and when I asked why, they said because they're sturdy, predictable, and very little trouble. If something does go wrong, Nikon's service to the White House is extraordinary. They'll rush over and repair things in an instant or provide a replacement.

Ronald Reagan creates a kind of magic when he enters a crowded room. He's a tall, good-looking man, who carries himself beautifully, and can deliver a speech which sounds like he's making it up as he goes along even though he's reading every word off a teleprompter. This device consists of two see-through glass plates the size of folded newspapers standing on long pipes on either side of the president's lectern. The words of his speech move down both glass plates at the same speed, allowing him to look from side to side as he speaks, or down at the lectern, where he has a copy of the speech printed on cards. Quite a few people in the audience think the glass plates are there to protect him from an assassination attempt, further enhancing the feeling of spontaneity.

Ronald Reagan has a little bit of a limp, a kind of rolling gait, as the result of fracturing his leg back in the summer of 1949 when he was one of the highest-paid male stars in Hollywood, earning $169,000 a year, or more than twice as much as President Harry Truman. The fracture came during a charity baseball game benefiting the City of Hope Hospital between the Hollywood Leading Men (Reagan's team) and the Comedians, with Bob Hope on the mound. Reagan connected with one of Hope's pitches, hit it out of the infield, and took off like a shot for first base (he was thirty-eight at the time). But as he arrived, the first baseman fell on top of him, he heard an awful crunch, and knew his leg was broken. But the crowd, figuring it was all part of the fun, laughed and hollered as he was carried off the field. He ended up at Saint John's Hospital, where I later practiced, and had his leg put in traction for about eight weeks, which was the way you fixed broken limbs back then. Today we'd fix his leg with steel pins and he'd be back on his feet in a matter of days—yet another illustration, should it be needed, of the way the practice of medicine is constantly being improved.

The president had a good diet. Breakfast was usually orange juice, whole wheat toast, cereal, decaffeinated coffee, and sometimes fruit in season. He ate few eggs and used margarine instead of butter. For lunch he'd have cottage cheese, a salad, soup, and fruit which he ate at his desk in the Oval Office. On Thursdays he'd lunch with Vice President Bush in his private office next door, and when lunching with large groups he'd go to the Roosevelt Room across the hall. To guard against the president's food being poisoned, it was randomly purchased at different stores by White House personnel wearing civilian clothes and driving unmarked cars.

The president and First Lady, considering their ceremonial obligations, ate a surprising number of evening meals in the privacy of their White House living quarters, where the menu was usually fish or chicken, with red meat perhaps once a week. The president would occasionally sip a little wine with his dinner (and never smoked). As his doctor, I can say his diet satisfied me.

Members of the president's cabinet and others would occasionally invite nationally known experts to lunch in the Cabinet Room, where they'd brief Mr. Reagan about new developments on the cutting edge of their various disciplines. Dr. Otis Bowen, secretary of health, education and welfare, invited me to sit in on one briefing by an outstanding group of surgeons, internists, cardiologists, immunologists, and other specialists who told the president about the latest advances in medicine such as the litholotriptor, which uses ultrasound to pulverize kidney stones thus eliminating the need for surgery; new techniques for lowering cholesterol, and a new anticancer drug called interleukin, whose efficacy had been blown all out of proportion by *Time* magazine.

At one point in the briefing I asked the doctors' advice on how the president should deal with interleukin, since it was being heralded as a great new cure for cancer, with the only supply, and a modest one at that, located at the National Institutes of Health in Bethesda, Maryland. People with cancer are desperate, and it reminded me of the old days when the king's subjects are starving, he has the only supply of food in the land, and they break down the castle gates to get it. Interleukin, however, has proved to be helpful only in cancer of the skin and kidney, and is not the cure-all so many originally thought it might be.

I think the president's good health also owes a lot to Nancy Reagan, who's been his wife and best friend since they were married in 1952. I'm sure he discussed his problems with her, the kind which beset every president. And this can be very therapeutic and very cathartic, as it lessens stress and is simply a happier way to live. He might have a trying day in the Oval Office, but the moment he stepped into the White House elevator to go home he'd begin to unwind.

The president would usually bring home a stack of work, take it into his study, and then change clothes and join the First Lady in the minigym in their quarters equipped with a stationary bicycle, treadmill, and weights, which they used religiously. "You've got to do it," the president always said, "because it's very easy to put off, and you can always find an excuse, so just do it."

At one point someone asked me to prepare a list of trained people who could give the president a massage up in his quarters, but it never amounted to anything. If an acceptable masseur or masseuse had been found, the Secret Service would have assigned an agent to be with the president when he was getting massaged, just like they did when someone from the outside came in to adjust his hearing aid.

The president and First Lady would finish their workout, shower, often put on their pajamas and bathrobes, and eat dinner off trays in front of the television set in the president's study overlooking the

South Lawn with the Jefferson Memorial and Washington Monument in the background. The president would also read, write memos, and get his night's work done before he and Mrs. Reagan retired sometime after 10:30 P.M.

President Reagan was sensible about getting proper rest. I know he never took naps at Camp David or his ranch, and never took sleeping pills. He did nod off once during a meeting with Pope John Paul II at the Vatican in Rome, but that was attributed to jet lag. Not long after that, the length of his rest stops was increased when he traveled overseas so he could adjust his biological clock (it takes about one day for each time zone you pass through). After a trip to Tokyo, which exhausted us all including the rugged Secret Service men, the president quipped, "Let's not travel East to West anymore, just North and South so we won't get jet lagged."

I was gratified again by the steps we took to protect President Reagan against jet lag when I read about how President Bush had verbally stumbled during a whirlwind trip he took to Asia a month after his inauguration. He had had no rest stops on his trip from Washington to Tokyo to attend Hirohito's funeral, then on to Beijing for a meeting with China's top leaders, and finally to Seoul, South Korea, where he mangled a speech to the National Assembly, saying things like "the last members of the Olympic flame" instead of "last embers."

President Bush apparently overdid it again following the July 4th, 1990, holiday at his Maine retreat where press reports said he went nonstop "throwing horseshoes, casting fishing lures, bashing golf balls, and careening across the waves in his speedboat" almost up to the time he left on a six-hour night flight across the Atlantic to attend a meeting in London of the Atlantic alliance. The then sixty-six-year-old president "got off Air Force One looking tired, eyes puffy and his stride less spry than the 'spring colt' to which he always compared himself," and then went right into a meeting with other heads of state. I'm sure most White House physicians would like to see their president arrive a day early for such meetings in order to get over jet lag and rest up a bit. But with the president of the United States, that's often easier said than done.

Making Life Easy

Everything is done to make the president's life as comfortable and stress free as possible. He's surrounded by literally hundreds of helpers whose sole job is to do things for him so he won't have to waste his priceless time doing them for himself. There was a barber shop in the West Wing of the White House for the exclusive use of the president, whose hair was cut by Milton Homer Pitts, who looks a lot like famed California trial lawyer Melvin Belli. Pitts numbers among his other celebrity clients Presidents Richard Nixon, Gerald Ford, and now George Bush, but not Jimmy Carter, whose hair, he claims, was trimmed by Mrs. Carter's hairdresser. Pitts and his manicurist would leave his four-chair, marble-floored shop in the Sheraton-Carlton Hotel and walk the few steps to the White House whenever he was summoned by the president. There was also a dental office in the White House basement manned by a Navy captain who reported to me and came in once or twice a week to mainly look after the Reagans and Bushes.

The president's secretary, Kathy Osborne, was located in a surprisingly small area directly outside the Oval Office which contains a bank of telephone lines capable of putting the president in virtually instant touch with almost anyone he needed to reach anywhere on the planet. The president had direct lines to the Central Intelligence Agency and the Pentagon, secure lines where his calls can be scrambled (so they'd sound like gobbledygook to anyone listening in), and a private line for his personal use. All telephone lines serving the Oval Office go through the White House switchboard in the basement of the Old Executive Office Building next door, which is run by a fabulous group of operators. Legend has it that these women can track down anyone the president and members of his staff need to reach. I don't doubt it, because they never failed to find me, although I tried to be helpful by always wearing a beeper and giving them a copy of my itinerary whenever I could. White House telephone operators also have a wonderful ear for voices. It's been several years since I worked there, yet they'll usually greet me by name whenever I call in.

The centerpiece in President Reagan's Oval Office was a desk given to the United States by Britain's Queen Victoria. The desk was made out of timbers from the British warship HMS *Resolute*, which was rescued by the U.S. Navy after being stuck in the ice near the Arctic Circle. The president loved this desk, even though it was too low for him to get his knees under when sitting on the chair he had brought with him from his governor's office in California. The poor man had to sit sideways when using this desk, so one time when he was away, enterprising staff members had a four-inch riser installed on the bottom of the desk so he could get his knees under it and work comfortably. This little gesture really touched him when he returned to the Oval Office.

If there was a party going on at the White House, the president and First Lady would wait until the last minute to come down from their quarters, and then go back upstairs as soon as dinner was over and they had danced with their honored guests as they did, for example, at a banquet for England's next king and queen. On that occasion, the First Lady danced with Prince Charles, and the president with the beautiful Lady Diana, who had asked that several young dancers be invited including movie actor John Travolta. After Travolta had danced with Lady Diana, he hurried into the White House Red Room to catch his breath, came up to Kit and me, who happened to be standing there, and in an excited voice said, "I'm so nervous. I just danced with a real princess!"

The minute the president and First Lady leave a White House banquet, everybody goes. The wonderful Marine orchestra is still playing away, the bar and the food are still there, but the only ones on the dance floor are usually three or four senior staff couples like Kit and me who had the entire place to ourselves.

The president and First Lady remained in the White House over Christmas so as not to inconvenience the dozens of staff people (and their families) who would have had to accompany them if they left Washington. But as soon as Christmas was over, they'd fly off to sunny California and the annual New Year's party given by their longtime friends Mr. and Mrs. Walter Annenberg at their "Sunnylands" estate in the Palm Springs area.

Christmas was filled with White House receptions, and the president and First Lady would vary their appearances at them. If it was a large reception they might simply walk down the stairs from their living quarters, give everyone a wave and warm Christmas greeting, and go back up again. If it was a smaller reception, the Reagans might stand at the head of a receiving line where they could shake hands and be photographed with guests. And for a senior staff party they would mix, mingle, and chat, and then line up for photographs in front of the White House Christmas tree.

I had some medical reservations about the president and First Lady greeting so many people during the winter flu season. But they handled it very well and never became ill even though the president told me he'd shake 75,000 hands before Christmas was over. One reason the president never became ill may have been because we had him carefully wash his hands after each round of holiday greetings.

Chapter Seven

"The Four Golden Minutes"

Air Force One would frequently fly over George Washington's Mt. Vernon home as it carried Ronald Reagan on one of his many trips away from the capital. I often wondered what America's first president would think if he could look up and see the big silver bird today's presidents use to get around, a big change compared to the horse that was state of the art in his day.

Yet everyone aboard Air Force One was nonchalant about the whole thing unless they were dealing with a crisis. People read, listened to tapes, wrote memos, worked on their laptop computers, talked, or slept. But when there was a crisis, like the terrorist capture of the cruise ship *Achille Lauro* in which an American was killed, Air Force One would become a hotbed of activity. President Reagan and his top aides would gather in the plane's conference room, the door would be shut, messages would be passed in and out, and you could feel the electricity in the air.

I looked after a few people aboard Air Force One, but never anything more serious than a dizzy spell or upset stomach. I never worried too much about members of the press riding in the rear of the plane because they were all fairly young and healthy. But I did get alarmed when the president invited older senators aboard for a trip across the United States. This was particularly true when I wasn't told in advance about any medical problems they might have. I had no idea if they were diabetic or had heart trouble—nothing. I was most concerned during long trips over the Atlantic and Pacific oceans when we might be airborne for eight hours or more with the nearest hospital emergency room possibly several thousand miles away. I was it, and it worried me.

One man who had the information I needed about President Reagan's congressional guests aboard Air Force One was the medical director for the U.S. Congress, Admiral William Narva, M.D. I worked closely with him whenever the president was scheduled to go up to the Hill to visit the House or Senate, and he agreed that he could provide me with cogent, confidential medical information about any member of Congress I might be called upon to treat in an emergency. But I left the White House before anything was done, and I presume the idea was dropped.

My Greatest Surprise

I was constantly amazed at the effort that goes into protecting the president of the United States as he's moved from one place to another. People wonder why the president can't drop in on their little meeting and say hi, or why he can't visit their church on Sunday morning. The answer is that it takes countless hours of security checks before the president is allowed to leave the White House in his limousine or helicopter, or depart for an overseas trip aboard Air Force One with the Stars and Stripes illuminated on its tail. I felt far safer flying with the president, by the way, than on any regularly scheduled airline, because I knew the maintenance on Air Force One, as well as the preflight security check for explosives, was the most exhaustive in the world.

"Preadvancing" the President

The planning for presidential trips frequently begins several months in advance. A "preadvance" team including one of the White House nurses leaves first to find out exactly what the presidential party will be dealing with. The nurse reports back to me on the adequacy of both emergency and definitive care for the president and his party, which may run into hundreds of people. I would occasionally attend a meeting of the president's staff to outline the medical risks of taking him to out-of-the-way places such as the West Indies island of Grenada; Mexicali, Mexico; or the island of Bali, at the end of the medical world. I vehemently protested a stopover in Bali, but was told it was on and that I'd have to make it work—and I did even though it continued to worry me.

The "preadvance" team is followed a few months later by an "advance" team, which actually sets things up in an effort to make sure that everything goes off without a hitch. The next trip is the real thing, and if the president is traveling overseas he's usually shown videos of the foreign leaders he's going to meet, taught how to pronounce their names phonetically, and briefed on highlights of their countries' history, economics, and politics.

Several hundred people usually accompany the president on trips abroad, from the doctor and "football" man, who travel with him aboard Air Force One, to Eddie Serrano, who's been majordomo to five presidents and flies in a backup plane with the rest of the party. One of Eddie's jobs was to bring along the president's food and water so he wouldn't get an upset stomach from a "bug" in the local drinking water, which could throw the whole trip off schedule. So could the loss of the president's contact lenses, his backup reading glasses, or batteries for his two hearing aids, for which he and I always carried extra supplies.

I also carried six pints of blood with me whenever we left the White House on a trip in case the president was injured and needed an immediate transfusion. The blood had been pretested to make certain it was not contaminated with the AIDS virus, hepatitis, or syphilis, and was kept refrigerated in the infirmary at Camp David, in my trailer at the Reagan ranch, and in a dry-ice container aboard Air Force One. The only time we stockpiled frozen supplies of the president's own blood was when we had scheduled surgery on him and knew he might require transfusions. We did this right before I left in early 1987 when we were getting ready for his prostate operation. Stockpiling blood is a commonplace medical procedure performed daily in private hospitals throughout the country. We did not keep an emergency blood supply on hand for the First Lady since she was not a likely target of a shooter's bullets.

"The Four Golden Minutes"

The first thing I looked at when the president was planning a trip abroad was the quality of the local medical facilities. I was rarely satisfied and would usually beef them up prior to the president's arrival. I wanted to be prepared to take advantage of what emergency room doctors call "The Four Golden Minutes" when you can frequently save a life—or lose it—following a heart attack, stroke, accident, or gunshot wound. You need to give the patient immediate attention during those precious few minutes. Then, after you have the patient stabilized, you need to provide definitive care.

When I heard the president had been shot in the chest by John W.

Hinkley, Jr., outside the Washington Hilton, I knew exactly what would happen if he didn't receive fast medical attention. The president would bleed into his chest, his lungs wouldn't be able to expand, he'd become short of breath, and if something wasn't done he'd "drown" in his own blood. The doctor's job was to quickly get a tube into his chest to drain off the blood so his lungs could expand and he could breathe.

Then the president would have to be rushed to a definitive care hospital where a surgeon would stop the bleeding, and explore his lung to see if it had been punctured. If it had, the surgeon would suture the hole to control bleeding and prevent the escape of air into the pleural space between the president's lung and the chest wall. He might also remove a portion of his damaged lung before suturing the wound and sending him off to a recovery room. The surgeon would then search for the bullet that had punctured the president's lung, but might decide not to remove it unless it's easy to recover. In the old days, as we've seen, they used to probe for the bullet, but surgeons rarely do that anymore. Today, physicians often depend on standard X-rays and CAT scans to "radiographically explore" patients with gunshot wounds.

The number one medical problem we faced during presidential trips abroad was where we could take him, or members of his party, to get definitive medical care.

When the president scheduled a one-day trip to the tiny island of Grenada more than a year after the U.S. invasion, dubbed "Operation Urgent Fury," we checked the local medical facilities and found them to be extremely primitive. So we created our own definitive care capability right there, because the closest first-class hospital was in Miami, and it would have taken nearly three hours to get him there in Air Force One. So I had a helicopter landing ship, a kind of baby aircraft carrier, stationed less than ten minutes offshore. It had an excellent medical setup which we augmented with extra doctors, laboratory and X-ray equipment. One concern was that members of the president's party might be involved in an accident since the Grenadians drive their cars and motorbikes like crazy along the island's narrow dirt roads with little traffic control.

Handling Emergencies Aboard Air Force One

I hadn't taken more than two or three trips with the president aboard Air Force One when I began upgrading my ability to save his life should he have a heart attack or stroke, or be injured while in the air. These were my main concerns, since I had already made sure the president was in good health before stepping out of the White House.

One of the first things I did was to replace the two little oxygen bottles which were kept within easy reach aboard Air Force One with a full five-foot-tall tank of oxygen which might be needed to keep the president alive during a long flight over the ocean. This upset some people because they had no place to hang their coat in the closet on Air Force One so I'd have room for the oxygen tank and a long tube which could reach all the way to the president's private quarters, consisting of two rooms plus bath near the front of the plane. But I insisted it be done, and it was.

The biggest thing I lacked on Air Force One was help. I fought desperately, and even gave a live, simulated team resuscitation drill to demonstrate the need for an additional medical person aboard. But it was decided not to bump a political type in order to free up a seat for another doctor or a nurse. With a nurse I could have handled almost anything; by myself I'm not so sure. If the president's heart began fibrillating wildly (which can mean death in minutes), I'd be trying to reassure him, the First Lady, and others as I was rushing to hook him up to my automatic defibrillator to get his heart beating normally again. If he had a heart attack, I'd be hovering over him, but would need someone to take an electrocardiogram and transmit it to cardiologists at the Bethesda Naval Hospital via the plane's telemetry gear so they could give me their opinion. I ended up training the president's military aides to handle the communications part of my job since I couldn't do everything myself.

One feature of Air Force One which worried me a great deal was the small size of the quarters where I'd have to treat the president if he had a heart attack or stroke, or had a piece of food stuck in his throat requiring me to do a tracheotomy (inserting a tube into his windpipe through an incision in the front of his neck to prevent suffocation). Ronald Reagan is a big man, six feet one and nearly 200 pounds. Realistic drills showed that after you've squeezed him, me, the First Lady, and a couple of Secret Service men into his small bedroom it would be very uncomfortable and impossible to do good work. Air Force One was upgraded from a 707 to a far more spacious 747 in 1991, which should make it possible to take much better care of the president and his party. My only regret is that I wasn't around when this huge new plane was delivered.

A presidential 747 that I was able to inspect, and it was a most unsettling experience, was the specially equipped National Emergency Command Airborne Post (NECAP) (pronounced "kneecap") from which the president would attempt to run the country following a nuclear missile attack. The president, his top aides, and I would leave our loved ones behind in what might be an atomic wasteland. We'd then fly above the devastation as the president struggled to learn how badly the country had been hurt, what could be done to aid the survivors, and how best to answer the aggressor. My job was to look after the president, and decide whether the outside air was contaminated with deadly radiation or was fit to breathe, before allowing anyone to leave the plane upon landing.

Landing the President in Case of Emergency

As I was flying across the country on Air Force One, I realized I knew nothing about where to land in case of an onboard medical emergency. So I went to the pilot and asked how long it would take to get the president down on the ground while flying at 36,000 feet. He said twenty minutes to land the plane within a one-hundred-mile radius of the point where he began his descent. So I gave instructions to the military people that the next time the president took a trip aboard Air Force One, I wanted to have a map pinpointing the location of every hospital within one hundred miles of our flight path that had an advanced trauma life support unit. I also told them I wanted the map to list each hospital's telephone number, the name of its head doctor, and the time it would take one of its ambulances to dash from the airport to the hospital.

The American College of Surgeons compiled a list of all the hospitals with acceptable acute trauma care units, which we used as a guide. We quickly learned that there were relatively few civilian hospitals with these facilities in many of the lightly populated southwestern states, but fortunately there was usually a military hospital enroute so we were covered. Still, I always felt a little more comfortable when we finally passed the Rocky Mountains and were approaching the coast of California, where there are plenty of good hospitals.

All the time we spent preparing to handle emergencies involving the president, by the way, was done without his knowledge; we were simply doing our job.

Five Historic Days in West Germany

President Reagan's schedule for Tuesday, April 30, 1985, read simply: *N* 9:30 Depart for Bonn*. Translated, this meant the president, accompanied by Nancy Reagan (N) would leave the White House (*) on their way to Bonn, West Germany. They'd be accompanied by Secretary of State George Shultz, Treasury Secretary James Baker, Chief of Staff Don Regan, Special Assistant Jim Kuhn, Press Spokesman Larry Speakes, the military aide with the "football," two Secret Service agents, and me.

We'd all walk out of the diplomatic entrance and onto the South Lawn as television lights were switched on, news photographers' strobe lights flashed, a crowd of well-wishers applauded, last-minute good-byes were said, and those of us manifested to ride with the president boarded HMX1. The helicopter's big rotor blades quickly lifted us into the air for a spectacular ten-minute flight past the Washington Monument, over the Jefferson Memorial, and then east down the Potomac River to Andrews Air Force Base, where Air Force One would be waiting for our overnight flight to Bonn.

At 11:10 A.M. on Wednesday, May 1, 1985, Air Force One touched down at the Bonn/Cologne airport in West Germany for five of the most historically significant days of Ronald Reagan's eight years as president of the United States.

The main reason for the trip was President Reagan's participation in the Bonn economic summit attended by the leaders of the world's seven leading industrialized nations. This was strictly business: familiar and pleasantly routine. What followed was the president's brief encounter with the horrors of Adolf Hitler's Germany, ceremonial visits to the Bergen-Belsen concentration camp, where thousands of innocent people were put to death, and then on to the World War II military cemetery in Bitburg, where German soldiers are buried, including some who were members of Hitler's dreaded Waffen SS elite guard.

The 1985 economic summit brought together the heads of Britain, Canada, France, Italy, Japan, West Germany, and the United States, who spent two days discussing critical economic problems buffeting their countries, from the slowing of the American economy and the strength of the U.S. dollar to high unemployment in Europe and Japan's flooding of foreign markets with its cars, TVs, VCRs, and other products (while aggressively protecting its own market against foreign goods).

Our presidential party left Air Force One and jammed ourselves into a small Huey helicopter for the brief flight across the Rhine River, past the historic city of Bonn dominated by its majestic Münster cathedral, and out over the countryside to the Schloss Gymnich castle which the West German government uses as a guest house. After briefly inspecting the castle's accommodations, I reviewed the German medical team and the ambulance which I had put on twenty-four-hour standby. I was both amazed and delighted by the country's medical facilities, which were first-class.

West Germany, for example, is covered with a web of high-speed autobahns, and as a doctor I was intrigued by the fact that they go through long stretches of barren countryside miles from the nearest hospital emergency room. Cars race along these highways at up to 130 miles an hour, and when an accident occurs it's apt to be catastrophic. To deal with this situation, the Germans have developed mobile emergency rooms which are driven to the scene of an accident and manned by an anesthesiologist and an assistant.

The anesthesiologist checks the accident victim's vital signs, provides an airway for breathing, starts intravenous fluids to treat shock, relieves pain with medication, and, if necessary, can even give an anesthetic to a person trapped in a wrecked automobile. The mobile emergency room is then driven to the nearest medical center where the unit—with doctor and patient inside—is lifted off the truck bed into a hospital bay and carried inside where treatment continues without missing a beat. To reduce wasted motion to a minimum, everything in the unit is color coded: bright red for equipment involving the heart or bleeding; green for breathing; and yellow for everything else.

The Price of Friendship

West German Chancellor Helmut Kohl had asked President Reagan to attend a wreath-laying ceremony at the Kolmeshohn military cemetery in Bitburg during the summit, and Mr. Reagan had readily agreed. The president liked Kohl, and wanted to demonstrate the war was over, and that the United States and Germany were now close friends and allies. Others including most members of the U.S. House and Senate, Jewish organizations, and veterans' groups, were horrified by the idea.

What horrified them was that while Mike Deaver himself had been sent ahead to do the advance work on the summit, he had failed to discover that 49 of the 2,000 or so German soldiers buried at Bitburg were members of the Waffen SS. Jewish historian and winner of the Nobel Peace Prize Elie Wiesel, whose mother, father, and sister had been murdered by the Nazis in Jewish death camps, begged President Reagan not to visit Bitburg, and condemned the trip after he went.

President Reagan tried to balance things by first visiting the grave of West Germany's revered first chancellor, Konrad Adenauer, which had been suggested by the evangelist Billy Graham. The president and Chancellor Kohl then flew on Air Force One to Hannover, and transferred to one of the Huey helicopters we had brought over for the fifteen-minute flight to the Jewish concentration camp at Bergen-Belsen, where some 50,000 victims of the Nazi terror are buried in mass graves covered with heather. One of them is Anne Frank, the Dutch girl who wrote an inspiring diary of the more than one year she spent with her family hiding in an attic in Amsterdam before being discovered by the Nazis and put to death at Bergen-Belsen.

As the president and First Lady walked through the entrance to the death camp, they passed a sign reading "Visitors are requested to observe the dignity of these memorial grounds and refrain from disturbing the peace of the dead." President Reagan placed a wreath of green ferns in front of a memorial obelisk in the camp with a ribbon from the "People of the United States." During his remarks, the president said, "Here death ruled. But we have learned something as well. Because of what happened, we found that death cannot rule forever. And that is why we are here today." Later he noted that just three weeks before Anne Frank was captured by the Nazis and sent to Bergen-Belsen to die at age fourteen, she had written in her diary: "It's really a wonder that I haven't dropped all my ideals, because they seem so absurd and impossible to carry out. Yet I keep them, because in spite of everything I still believe that people are really good at heart."

The Huey helicopter carrying President Reagan, Chancellor Kohl, and the rest of our party lifted out of a cordon of hundreds of West German police and U.S. Secret Service agents who had sealed off Bergen-Belsen for the ride back to Hannover and the 200-mile flight south to the U.S. Air Force Base at Bitburg. We arrived around midday as a band played, and hundreds of people on the ground waved American and West German flags as Air Force One taxied to a stop. We piled into a waiting motorcade, and were driven a few miles to the Kolmeshohn cemetery in the town's western suburbs, where we were met by U.S. and German honor guards.

The ensuing ceremony was simplicity itself. There were no speeches. The president, wearing a bullet-proof raincoat, walked to a brick tower surrounded by the graves of German soldiers and laid a wreath next to it. This time the ribbon read from the "President of the United States," and not the "People of the United States." The entire occasion lasted a mere eight minutes.

Weeks before we left for Europe, the White House switchboard had received a call from a man who said he was General Matthew B. Ridgeway, and would like to help President Reagan any way he could during his upcoming visit to Bitburg, which was already being heralded by the media as a diplomatic disaster.

The White House operator put Ridgeway through to a member of the president's staff who recognized him immediately. The ninety-year-old general had been chief of staff of the U.S. Army, commander of the North Atlantic Treaty Organization (NATO), and leader of the 82nd Airborne Division, which fought in the Battle of the Bulge, the last major German offensive of the war, in which many of the German troops buried at Bitburg had lost their lives.

President Reagan invited General Ridgeway to stand beside him during the wreath-laying ceremony at the Kolmeshohn cemetery. Chancellor Kohl's staff was notified, and Kohl asked retired German air ace Lieutenant General Johannes Steinoff, seventy-one, to be his escort at Bitburg. After the wreath was laid, and a moment of silence observed, the two old generals shook hands, and the past was left to rest in peace.

A happier event took place the next day, when the Reagans and the Kohls helicoptered *up* the Rhine River from Bonn to Hambrach Castle, where President Reagan was to deliver a major address.

People continue to ask me what I felt was the most unusual experience during my time at the White House, and I have to believe this was very special. Here I was with two leading heads of state and their wives together in a small helicopter along with the military aide and Jim Kuhn. The Rhine River never looked better, the vineyards never looked greener, and the castles on the crests of the hills were never more dramatic.

The arrival at Hambach Castle was spectacular, and the president spoke to some 5,000 cheering students telling them at one point that from their ranks can come a new Bach, Beethoven, Goethe, or Otto Hahn (a renowned German physical chemist). The students gave the president a book on German history, and serenaded him with "The Star-Spangled Banner."

As the motorcade headed back to the heliport, and we were all still wrapped in the warm glow of this moment, someone yelled, "My God, do you see that!" I immediately looked out the car window and saw we were being "mooned" by three young Germans who had stuck out their bare bottoms at us while holding up a sign in English reading "Reagan Go Home." "Are they hes or shes?" somebody asked, and being a doctor and familiar with such things, I said, "From the rear you can't tell."

Visiting the King and Queen of Spain

At 1:40 P.M. on Monday, May 6, President and Mrs. Reagan flew out of the Ramstein Air Base in West Germany enroute to Madrid, Spain, for a two-day visit with King Juan Carlos de Borbon and Queen Sophia.

It was a perfect day, with a blue Andalusian sky and puffy white clouds, and as Air Force One neared Madrid's Barajas Airport, advance man Bill Henkel suggested we get up a "wheels-in-blocks pool" much like the "anchor-down pool" on cruise ships. It was then 3:30 P.M., and Air Force One was scheduled to be on the ground with blocks under its wheels at 4:15 P.M. We didn't want any part of Henkel's little game because we knew Air Force One always landed exactly on time. The captain would build some "fat" into the landing schedule so he could speed up or slow down in order to taxi Air Force One to its prearranged stopping point precisely on time.

This never failed to impress the dignitaries, honor guard, bands, press corps, and hundreds of spectators standing there awaiting the president's arrival. I know this pageantry touched and inspired President Reagan whenever he visited a foreign country. It also helps explain why presidents are reluctant to leave office after the exhilaration of such moments, moments I experienced myself, as I always followed President Reagan out the forward door of Air Force One and into the midst of the cheering crowds gathered at the foot of the exit ramp.

I kept thinking of the days of hard work which had made this moment possible. Troops shining their shoes, polishing their brass, cleaning and checking their rifles, and drilling for hours so they'd be letter-perfect. I'm sure many of those in the receiving party had used all kinds of stratagems to wheedle an invitation to the dignitaries' enclosure. And when the day finally arrived, there was the dilemma of what to wear, where to stand to be seen to best advantage, how to figure who outranked whom in protocol—the list is endless.

Air Force One made a wide sweeping circle around Barajas Airport, landed at the far end of the runway, and taxied slowly and majestically toward its assigned stopping point (almost always the edge of a broad red carpet). We could hear the military band starting to play, and see the row of troops drawn up to attention with flags flying. There was the usual hullabaloo inside the plane as cabin attendants handed out coats and hats, and staff people gathered up their briefcases before leaving via the rear exit.

Julius Bengtsson, the First Lady's hairdresser, had gone forward to the president's cabin to give her a final comb out. Presidential assistant Jim Kuhn soon followed to remind the Reagans where they were to go, whom they were about to meet, and what was expected of them during the arrival ceremony now only minutes away. Jim had checked and double-checked every detail of these arrangements with our advance people on the ground minutes before briefing the Reagans.

A cabin attendant handed me my vest and coat which I put on as I pulled up my tie, ran a comb through my hair, and checked my wallet to make sure my diplomatic passport was in order. I then asked President Reagan's personal secretary, Kathy Osborne, if I looked "presidential," and when she assured me I did, I felt ready to step out of Air Force One. But before leaving, I retrieved my medical bag which I always carried in one hand, and slung my briefcase over my shoulder by its strap. This left me one hand free to hold on to the exit ramp when leaving the plane, for climbing into the presidential motorcade, and for instant use in case of a medical emergency. I was probably the only person who looked burdened and harried when exiting Air Force One, since I was loaded down with gear while everyone else had their hand luggage sent directly to their rooms.

The forward and rear doors of the big white and blue Boeing 707 were then flung open, admitting the sunny warm air of Spain. It all seemed vaguely familiar to me, and I'm sure to President Reagan too since we lived in southern California, which has a similar climate and a rich Spanish heritage. We make our home in Los Angeles (City of Angels), and are surrounded by reminders of our past such as the Camino Real (Highway of Kings) running from San Diego to Sonoma and dotted with twenty-one Spanish missions.

U.S. Air Force personnel were in position to guide the president's plane to its final stop, attach ground communications and air-conditioning equipment, and begin servicing the plane for its departure the next day. The first to leave from the plane's rear exit was the Presidential Protective Detail of ten men who quickly surrounded it as a security shield. Other U.S. agents already on the ground had secured the perimeter, and checked the arrival party for concealed weapons. I was met by nurses from my White House medical unit who had preadvanced the site, and worked with local medical people designated by the Spanish government in selecting the hospital we'd rush the president to in an emergency. The presidential motorcade was in position, as were White House staff people with mobile communications gear for use if needed during the president's brief walk from Air Force One to his motorcade for the drive to El Pardo Royal Palace.

Ten members of the White House press corps were on Air Force One, and they followed the Presidential Protective Detail out of the rear exit so they could get into position to see Ronald and Nancy Reagan as they emerged from the plane, waved to the crowd, and were greeted by King Juan Carlos and Queen Sophia.

As I waited with the president and First Lady to step out of Air Force One, men pushed the exit ramp up to the body of the plane and locked it securely in place so there'd be no accidents as we walked off. I could see myself giving President Reagan first aid with an army of waiting reporters and photographers recording it all for posterity. I kept thinking of those embarrassing pictures of President Gerald Ford, who bumped his head as he emerged from Air Force One and then slipped on the last step as he rushed to greet those rushing to greet him.

Ronald Reagan, like Jack Kennedy, had a natural presidential air about him, and his aides worked hard to keep it that way. No gaffs. No fluffs. And no stumbles when the unblinking eyes of hundreds of television and still cameras were recording his every move. The exit ramp had been designed by the Reagan White House with this in mind. It had an extra-wide platform on top, and as Air Force One's forward door with the great presidential seal on the inside swung open, the president and First Lady would step out onto this metal ministage and wave to the crowd below in a perfectly composed photo opportunity. The entire ramp had been covered with antiskid compound and equipped with sturdy handrails, and it always seemed to be there waiting no matter where Air Force One landed anywhere in the world.

This left the problem of the bottom step, which had tripped up President Ford. The Reagan White House defused this one by keeping welcoming parties well away from the stairs. The president and First Lady would finish getting ready in their quarters, emerge from the plane, wave to the crowd, come down the stairs, step onto the tarmac, and then walk over to greet the welcoming party being held back by our security people.

The U.S. ambassador to Spain, Thomas O. Enders, and our chief of protocol for Spain came aboard Air Force One to escort the president and First Lady to where the king and queen of Spain were waiting to greet them (the two couples had met several times before in Washington). President Reagan and King Juan Carlos strode side by side as they reviewed Spain's Royal Engineers standing at attention with picks, shovels, and saws strapped to their backs. The official party then walked directly to a sitting room in the modern glass and marble Royal Pavilion a few steps away. We members of the White House staff got into the waiting motorcade, followed by the president and King Juan Carlos, who entered the first limousine, with Mrs. Reagan and Queen Sophia in the one behind.

The signal "We have a departure" was radioed through the motorcade, and we were off on the twenty-minute ride to El Pardo Royal Palace, which had been Spain's royal residence for some four centuries. The palace was last occupied by Generalíssimo Francisco Franco until his death in 1975, and is used today as a museum and the official residence for visiting heads of state (much like our Blair House in Washington).

The motorcade stopped at the entrance to the palace garden, and the king and president with their wives were escorted to a dais. The national anthems of the United States and Spain were played, and the king then invited President Reagan to review the palace honor guard lined up along another red carpet leading back to the palace where the ladies were waiting. This provided another magnificent photo opportunity with the four of them standing in front of the palace, and the honor guard drawn up on either side with flags and banners waving in the evening breeze.

King Juan Carlos and Queen Sophia led the president and First Lady across a small bridge over a moat surrounding the old palace, and through its main door. Here they were introduced to officers of the royal guard and the administrator and housekeeper of the royal palace before being escorted up to the royal suite where the king and queen bid them adieu.

President Reagan was allowed to rest for one hour before meeting Spain's young Socialist Prime Minister Felipe González. The two leaders strolled out into the palace courtyard for a ten-minute "photo op" with the press, and then went back inside again for a forty-minute one-on-one meeting using "whisper interpreters." The interpreters knelt down beside the president and prime minister, who were seated facing each other, and whispered into their ears a running translation of what was being said. There was a multilingual notetaker present to record their conversation, which went off without a hitch (in part because of President Reagan's ability to imperceptibly adjust his hearing aids to catch every word spoken to him).

While all this was going on, I began looking around the palace so I'd know where things were in case of an emergency. The palace's ground floor contained the kitchen, cloakroom, caretaker's quarters, library, theater, chapel, entry rooms, and a museum. My room was next to President Reagan's, and as always I developed a contingency plan of how I would come to his aid in the event of a fire or other emergency. I usually left the door to my bedroom ajar so the Secret Service agent on duty outside the president's bedroom could rush in and wake me if I was needed.

My room in the palace was large and magnificently appointed with furniture of French design which had been handcrafted in the royal workshops, and an elegant mirrored bathroom of light green marble. A White House telephone had been placed in my room, and I immediately called the temporary White House switchboard installed in the palace to see if I was "on line." When I found I was, I asked one of the White House operators we had brought along to ring me to make sure I could receive incoming calls. I next checked my pocket pager to make sure I could be reached on my number 384, which followed me all over the world (for ease of communications, my nurses' numbers were 385 and 386).

It was easy for me to go visiting in the palace since all the rooms opened onto a central courtyard. Chief of Staff Don Regan's conference room with bedroom attached was to my right followed by Jim Kuhn's bedroom, the "football" aide's bedroom, and then President Reagan's reception room, office, dining room, and conference room, and the steward's preparation room.

As I was strolling around the palace courtyard getting acquainted, I saw an attractive young Spanish woman and decided to practice my southern California version of her native tongue. "Buenas tardes, señorita. ¿Qué pasa?" (Good afternoon, miss. What's going on?). As I braced myself for her answer in classic Spanish she said in perfect English, "Hi, my name is Maria, I'm your hostess, and I'm here to help you in any way I can. Do you need anything?"

I told her everything about El Pardo Royal Palace was perfect, but that I had been away from home for nearly a week and needed to get some laundry done. Maria disappeared, and in no time returned with a laundry hamper and a big basket of fruit. "Put your things in the hamper," she said, "and I'll have them back tomorrow. By the way, do you need any shopping done?" I said I could use some film and toothpaste, and handed her some dollars to pay for everything. "Doctor," she said, refusing the money, "it is the Spanish government's pleasure to have you as our guest and there will be no bill."

At 9 P.M. that night, I joined the president and First Lady for the five-minute motorcade drive to the home of King Juan Carlos and Queen Sophia, with whom they were having dinner. A small group of White House staffers accompanied the Reagans. The visit had been rehearsed by White House advance man Don Wegmiller, who had worked out all the details with the chief of the royal household. Jim Kuhn had briefed the Reagans on the evening ahead and would stand by until it was over. The military aide with the "football" was in overall charge of communications between the president and the outside world should they become necessary. Assistant Press Secretary Mark Weinberg was there to make sure the mob of reporters covering the visit stayed within the areas assigned to them, and to serve as the president's spokesman should the need arise. I was there with my nurse and emergency medical bags. But the heavy responsibility of coordinating the whole affair as far as the president and First Lady were concerned fell to chief advance man Bill Henkel, who pulled it off with no mistakes.

Guests in the Zarzuela Palace

The king and queen of Spain and their family live in the Zarzuela Palace, a small eighteenth-century building named after the light operas performed in the theater which used to occupy the site.

The president and First Lady were met as they stepped out of the motorcade by the chief of the royal household. The king and queen descended the steps of the Zarzuela Palace steps to welcome them, as a gaggle of waiting press photographers set off a shower of electronic flashes. Once inside the palace the Reagans were greeted by the king's and queen's two daughters: their Royal Highnesses Princesses Elena and Cristina (their only son and heir was away studying in Canada).

The president and First Lady were ushered into a reception room of the palace where they exchanged gifts with the king and queen before going into dinner. Just under an hour later, the two couples adjourned to the king's study for coffee. All of this was recorded by a White House photographer, and a short time later the king and queen received an album containing copies of the best of the pictures.

We members of the president's staff were brought in through a side door to the palace, and into a reception room where a table had been beautifully set for dinner with the food, wine, and dessert decidedly up to royal standards. After dinner we were invited to tour part of the small palace filled with works of art, along with family pictures and memorabilia. The highlight for me was the collection of silver ship models, and more importantly, silver trophies won by Queen Sophia, who is an accomplished sailor.

The Reagans said their good-byes to their hosts at 10:30 P.M., we all climbed into the motorcade, and five minutes later were back at El Pardo Royal Palace for a night's sleep before flying to Strasbourg, France, where President Reagan was to address the European Parliament, which is the world's only directly elected multinational deliberative body. When we were there it had representatives from ten countries, but was preparing to admit two more—Spain and Portugal.

President Reagan had been asked to speak to representatives of the ten Common Market countries on the fortieth anniversary of VE Day. "We mark today," President Reagan told the assembled diplomats, "the anniversary of the liberation of Europe from tyrants who had seized this continent and plunged it into a terrible war." The president then went on to discuss East-West tensions, the need to reduce them, and his hope that in the twenty-first century people and ideas will be able to travel freely "from Moscow to Lisbon," a hope that today seems well on its way to becoming a reality.

President Reagan's speech got off to a wobbly start when his teleprompter went on the blink causing him to pause, and skip entire sentences in his prepared text. To make matters worse, communist and leftist hecklers laughed and booed during the speech, and about two dozen walked out. After a reception and lunch, the president and First Lady climbed back aboard Air Force One for the 1,200-mile flight to Lisbon, Portugal.

Journey's End in Portugal

By the time we reached Lisbon and journey's end after nine hectic days in West Germany, France, and Spain, and now Portugal, we were all close to exhaustion. At one point a group of reporters and photographers traveling with us asked seventy-four-year-old President Reagan if he was tired. Flashing them a broad grin, the president said, "No, not at all, I've got youth on my side." But we were all drained to the point where Chief of Staff Don Regan was heard murmuring "I need a Coke. I need the caffeine. I need something to keep me going." And driving back from a lunch for the president at Sintra Castle, Press Spokesman Larry Speakes said the entire European trip was probably the most difficult of the Reagan presidency.

Portuguese President Antonio Ramalho Eanes was waiting to greet the Reagans as they descended from Air Force One, and to escort them to a formal arrival ceremony at the nearby Jeronimos Monastery. Portuguese Prime Minister Mario Soares, whom the president had met before, was standing among a group of government officials, but Mr. Reagan failed to recognize him. President Eanes instantly realized what had happened, and led Mr. Reagan back to greet Mr. Soares.

I've always been amazed at the hundreds of names and faces President Reagan had to remember, and did remember with rare exceptions. It reminds me of New York Governor Nelson Rockefeller, who was later vice president in the Ford Administration, and had so much trouble remembering names that he greeted practically everyone with "Hi, fella." On one occasion, Governor Rockefeller had to introduce the minister who was going to give the invocation at a black-tie dinner in New York City. Everyone waited with bated breath to see if he'd remember the padre's name; he began, "Ladies and Gentlemen, it is an honor for me to introduce Reverend Clergy."

There was the usual round of receptions and dinners with time off which I used, among other things, to inspect a little ambulance the Portuguese had put at our disposal, which was the size of a small station wagon. The ambulance was so small that the Portuguese doctor assigned to us could barely squeeze into it, let alone two six-footers like the president and myself. So I had to ask for a larger ambulance, which was quickly provided.

It was in Lisbon that I was again reminded of what an amazing job is done, with absolutely no fanfare, by the White House Communications Agency. The military aide with the "football" and I were standing near the president's motorcade waiting for him to emerge from a meeting when I offhandedly asked Marine Major Peterson standing next to me, where the nearest White House telephone had been installed. Without missing a beat, he reached into a nearby shrub and handed it to me.

It was finally time to leave Europe and head for home and a day or two of rest and relaxation, which we felt we all richly deserved. Hours later Washington's Andrews Air Force Base appeared out of Air Force One's windows and we began getting ready to wrap up the final details of the trip, including an encounter with a U.S. Customs agent. He'd come on board to ask us to voluntarily declare anything we were bringing into the country on which duty had to be paid such as a watch I had bought in Geneva, Switzerland. The president and First Lady never had a moment for private shopping on any of their overseas trips and so had nothing to declare to the man from Customs.

Chapter Eight

"Reagan's Doctors Find Cancer"

"Reagan's Doctors Find Cancer" was the four-column headline in the July 16, 1985, *New York Times* following the president's surgery for a big, possibly cancerous polyp found in his colon three days earlier.

The chain of events leading to the discovery of this painless, but potentially deadly tumor began on March 8, 1985, during the first annual physical examination I organized for the then seventy-four-year-old president at the Naval Hospital in Bethesda.

Dr. Daniel Ruge, my predecessor, had conducted a similar examination in 1984 when several small, noncancerous polyps were found in the president's colon located in the lower half of the large intestine, which together with the small intestine forms what's commonly known as the bowel. I wanted to make sure no new polyps had formed in the president's colon which could have conceivably ended his life.

One of the preliminary tests I did on President Reagan in my White House Medical Office before going to Bethesda was to screen for cancer of the colon by giving him a Hemoccult® test for blood in the stool. If it was negative, I'd know it was pretty unlikely that he had colon cancer, which is found in about 150,000 Americans each year.

The president's Hemoccult® test was positive, which worried me. I knew from experience, though, that false positives are often caused by problems other than colon cancer. I decided to reduce the chance of a common one showing up by restricting the president's consumption of red meat, which can leave traces of blood in the stool.

A few weeks later, at the suggestion of Navy Commander Edward Cattau, chief of gastroenterology at Bethesda, I did six more Hemoccult® tests on the president, which were all negative. But I was still worried because Ronald Reagan had a history of polyps; a noncancerous one had been removed from his colon one year earlier. We

105

therefore went ahead and examined the lower part of his colon and found a small polyp. This was biopsied, and the report indicated no malignancy.

Dr. Cattau and I thought this polyp should be removed at some convenient time in the near future. But President Reagan had already scheduled the trip to the economic summit meeting in Bonn, West Germany, with Chancellor Helmut Kohl, with side trips to France, Spain, and Portugal. The day I selected was Friday, July 12, 1985.

Several days before the president was to enter the hospital, my assistant Dr. John Hutton and I walked over to Chief of Staff Don Regan's office and sat down around a conference table with him, presidential counsel Fred Fielding, and White House spokesman Larry Speakes to tell them what was about to happen. We discussed how a sedative we planned to give the president to control pain during the removal of the polyp would affect his ability to carry out his duties.

I said it would make President Reagan drowsy, but that he could be roused at any time even though he might feel as though he had just had two martinis. Speakes jumped on this, saying I was being flip, and then turned to Dr. Hutton for "a more scientific explanation." This led to a discussion of how some people could handle two martinis while others would get knocked on their ear after one. What I was trying to do, of course, was give Regan, Fielding, and Speakes a layman's description of the sedative's power.

This was critical since they had to decide whether or not to recommend to President Reagan that he turn his power over to Vice President Bush under Section 3 of the Twenty-fifth Amendment to the Constitution. The amendment says if the president declares in writing to the Congress that he is unable to discharge his duties, the vice president shall assume those duties until the president again declares himself able to carry on.

I had studied the Twenty-fifth Amendment, and felt it wasn't necessary to invoke it in this instance because I planned to stay with President Reagan throughout his recovery period in case I had to bring him up chemically by giving him an injection of Antilirium® or Narcan®, used to reverse the effects of Valium® or an opiate-type drug. This is a gray area, and I doubt if the president or anyone else could have been roused using these techniques, and then pass a complex test of mental acuity. But they certainly would be alert enough to make a major "go/no-go" decision. I'm not a historian, but I don't know of a single instance—including the Japanese attack on

Pearl Harbor—when a president had to make a life-or-death decision in a single day, let alone the few hours we were dealing with here.

Cocktails at 9 A.M.

Shortly after 9 A.M. on Friday, July 12, I joined the president in the Oval Office for a round of medicinal cocktails. I poured each of us a drink in long-stemmed wine glasses, and then downed the first one with him as he grimaced and said, "This stuff tastes awful." The cocktail was a citrus-tasting concoction called Golytely® that prepares the intestinal tract for the examination.

I accompanied the president and First Lady as they left the White House at 1:30 P.M., and got into their Marine helicopter on the White House lawn for the ten-minute flight to the Bethesda Naval Medical Center. They sat on both sides of a table next to a large window, with the president facing forward. As we circled around to make sure everything was ready for us down below, the president leaned over to me and shouted above the noise of the rotors, "How many times do you think we've been here?" I knew he had been to Bethesda more times than he liked to remember, so I said this would be a routine visit, not knowing what we were about to find when we examined him.

We landed on the hospital's helipad near busy Wisconsin Avenue, which the Secret Service had closed to traffic, and were hustled into the secure cocoon of the motorcade for the ten-second drive to a small door on a little-used side of the hospital. The president could have strolled there in two or three minutes. But he'd have had to run a gauntlet of wild-eyed reporters shouting questions at him, and would have been an easy target for a hidden sharpshooter like Lee Harvey Oswald, who picked off President John F. Kennedy as he rode through Dallas. The official autopsy on President Kennedy's body was performed at Bethesda, and never again would the Secret Service allow presidents of the United States to ride around in open limousines.

We had to take the president and First Lady through Bethesda's outpatient department to get to the examination room, so we cordoned it off with drapes so nobody could see who was passing through. We had considered clearing out the entire hospital, but quickly dismissed the idea because we knew it would have inconvenienced a lot of people and that would have upset the president.

The examination room itself was fairly small, and seemed even more so after it was crowded with the president, Dr. Cattau, who would do the procedure to remove the president's tiny polyp, Dr. Cattau's associate, myself, two nurses, and Secret Service agent Ray Shaddick.

The president was prepared for the examination we figured would take an hour or so by being given an intravenous sedative. Dr. Cattau then removed the polyp growing on the wall of the president's lower intestine by using a colonoscope. This is a long, flexible, fiber-optic instrument with tiny biopsy forceps that's inserted into the colon through the rectum, eliminating the need for open surgery. The growth, fortunately for the president, turned out to be an inflammatory pseudopolyp rather than a more cancer-prone adenomatous polyp.

A White, Glistening, Golf-Ball-Size Polyp

I had previously decided, and Dr. Cattau had agreed, that while President Reagan was sedated and his intestinal tract cleaned out with laxatives and fasting, we should seize the opportunity to look at the rest of his colon, which had not been examined since 1981. Dr. Catttau had advanced the colonoscope some three feet further along the president's colon when, lo and behold, he spotted a white, glistening polyp about the size of a golf ball (in his book *Speaking Out,* Larry Speakes erroneously described the polyp as being "big, black and ugly").

Dr. Cattau, myself, and others were able to look at the huge polyp through the colonoscope's eyepiece (as well as photograph it for the record). The discovery of this polyp came as a total surprise. I had taken a long shot, and it worked. The polyp, however, was far too big to be removed by the colonoscope's delicate biopsy forceps, and as I gazed at it I was appalled. I thought, how can this be? How will I tell Mrs. Reagan? What will the media say? And it's not fair that this should happen to the president. I was brought back to reality by Dr. Cattau, who said, "Well, let's get some biopsies and see what we have here."

Dr. Cattau then sent for Navy Captain Dale Oller, head of surgery at the Bethesda Naval Medical Center, and briefed him on what he had found. Dr. Oller looked at the polyp, and said it would have to be removed by open surgery. He said this, by the way, without knowing the results of the biopsy, a painstaking procedure under way in the hospital's pathology laboratory whose final results were not expected to be ready until some time later that day. The pathologist would take bits of tissue from the surface of the polyp. These would be stained with chemical dyes to show the cells more clearly under the microscope. They'd then be mounted on glass slides, and examined under a microscope to see if the structure of the tissue cells had changed, indicating the possible presence of cancer.

All I could think about was that we might have to operate on the president. We'd have to render him unconscious for several hours with a general anesthetic, make an abdominal incision, remove the polyp, and pray it wasn't cancerous (and hadn't already spread throughout his body).

The four tiny bites taken from the surface of the polyp were examined under the microscope, and each one turned out to be negative, suggesting it wasn't cancerous. But a polyp is like a mushroom. It has a head and a stalk, and although we had looked at pieces cut from various parts of its surface, we couldn't analyze it all, so Dr. Oller, Dr. Cattau, and I decided it would be prudent to remove it surgically. The tendency of some polyps is to become malignant, and if left long enough they will become malignant. And since colon cancer kills 60,000 Americans a year and is the second-leading cancer killer after lung cancer in men and breast cancer in women, it must be taken seriously. This was particularly so with Ronald Reagan, because cancer often runs in families and just ten days earlier his older brother Neil, then seventy-six, had been operated on for a cancer in the same area of the colon and was given only a 65 to 80 percent chance of living another five years.

I helped roll the president from his examination room bed onto a gurney for the ride across the hall to the recovery room. I stayed with the president, told him the examination was finished, and that he should rest while his sedation was wearing off and I was certain all was well.

I then joined Drs. Cattau, Oller, and Hutton, and the First Lady, who had already been briefed on the large polyp we had found in her husband's colon. As the five of us talked in a doctor's office which had been fixed up as a waiting room for the First Lady, I told her I didn't know whether the polyp was cancerous or not, but that we had to tell the president, and we had to do something about it.

Avoiding the Word "Cancer"

Mrs. Reagan didn't raise any questions, or want a second opinion. She simply said, "What do you think?" and I said, "It's not an emergency, but we do need to remove the suspicious polyp and see if it's spread to the rest of his abdomen." Mrs. Reagan said she wanted to tell her husband, So at about 3:30 P.M. the five of us trooped over to the recovery room where President Reagan was propped up in bed wide-awake. Mrs. Reagan sat on the bed, put her outstretched arms on either side of her husband, looked directly into his eyes, and told him we had found another polyp which was too large to remove "through normal channels" and would require open surgery.

So they had a choice, either go on to Camp David and do it on return or do it now. The only trouble with waiting was that Ronald Reagan would have to take Golytely® again and he said "No way—let's do it."

Today's naval hospital in Bethesda is a modern 500-bed facility, but the presidential suite is still located in the old original part of the hospital which is no longer in use. The building was the brainchild of President Franklin D. Roosevelt, who actually drew a sketch of the hospital he wanted built, including its soaring central tower copied after the state capitol in Lincoln, Nebraska, that had caught his eye on a trip out there.

The presidential suite is loaded with communications equipment and reserved for the president's personal use even though he may never use it from one year to the next (there's a similar one on constant standby at the Walter Reed Army Medical Center). The presidential suite at Bethesda consists of a small sitting room, a large bedroom, a guest bedroom, bedrooms for the president's doctor and the military aide with the "football," a cabinet room for meetings, a treatment room, an office, and a galley where Eddie Serrano prepared meals for the Reagans and the military aide who had to be near the president at all times. (I had my meals in the hospital dining room downstairs.)

I have a lot of respect for Nancy Reagan, who was obviously distraught by the news of her husband's cancer. But she's a determined lady, all 106 pounds of her, and well versed in medical matters as I was reminded again a few months after I left the White House when a suspicious breast lesion was discovered on a routine mammogram. She was presented with three options (1) lumpectomy and radiation (2) do nothing and observe it or (3) if positive do a modified radical mastectomy. After considering all aspects of her schedule, age, and radiation effects she concluded to proceed with the modified radical surgery. She told the president, "It's my turn now. You've had yours, now I'll have mine." I think Mrs. Reagan will be all right. She had insisted on having physical checkups every six months, so her cancer was found very early and there's every chance her surgery removed it all.

Preparing the President for Surgery

The evening before we went after the president's large polyp, we put an intravenous in his arm, and I pushed him along in a wheelchair to the X-ray department where we did a series of preoperative tests on him including some baseline blood work and a CAT scan to see if there was any suggestion of a tumor in his lungs or abdomen.

This was the first time President Reagan had undergone this type of examination so I sat at his side and carefully explained how the CAT scan machine would take a series of X rays—like "slicing a loaf of bread"—from the lower abdomen to his neck. Since the president was a great reader, I managed to find a magazine which kept him occupied while the series was being completed. I knew he was restless, but he never complained.

It was now approaching midnight and I knew the president was getting tired. But I decided to keep going because the results were perfect, and the test was nearly completed when a huge thunder and lightning storm broke over the hospital. We were very concerned that we'd lose our computerized data and have to do the president's CAT scan all over again. But "Reagan luck" was with us and all was well.

We then set to work assembling an operating team, and decided to use both military and civilian doctors. I didn't want all Navy surgeons from Bethesda because it was under a cloud of suspicion due to reports of malpractice, and there was a loss of credibility. The Navy had accused Dr. Donald M. Billig, Bethesda's former top heart surgeon, of bungling the surgery on several patients, resulting in their death, and there were other serious patient problems as well. But they appeared to be isolated incidents, and did not shake my faith in Bethesda as the best possible place to perform surgery on President Reagan.

The medical team we organized consisted of seven doctors: four who would handle the surgery, and three of us who would be there as observers and, if called upon, as consultants. The surgical team was led by Dr. Oller, who would actually perform the operation, assisted by Dr. Lee E. Smith, a leading colon cancer surgeon at George Washington University Hospital; Navy Commander Bimal Ghosh, Bethesda's head of surgical oncology (the removal of tumors), and Dr. Hutton. I was there with Dr. Cattau and Dr. Stephen Rosenberg, chief of the surgery branch of the National Cancer Institute in Bethesda.

Mrs. Reagan arrived at the hospital at around 9 A.M. on July 13. The president was dressed in a green hospital gown and had his usual national security briefing, and meetings with Don Regan and Fred Fielding. Fielding had reviewed with Dr. Oller the upcoming operation on President Reagan, and as presidential counsel made the historic decision that Mr. Reagan's powers should be temporarily turned over to George Bush via a letter citing the provisions of the Twenty-fifth Amendment without actually invoking it so as not to set a precedent for future presidents. In her book *My Turn*, Mrs. Reagan said, "This was the first time the provisions of the Twenty-fifth Amendment had ever been put into effect," unaware that it had been sidestepped.

At 10:32 A.M., a half hour before we took President Reagan into the operating room, he signed two identical letters for delivery to Speaker Pro Tem of the U.S. Senate Strom Thurmond of South Carolina and Speaker of the U.S. House of Representatives Thomas P. O'Neill of Massachusetts. The letters making George Bush acting president of the United States read:

> I am about to undergo surgery during which time I will be briefly and temporarily incapable of discharging the constitutional powers and duties of the office of the President of the United States.
>
> After consultation with my Counsel and the Attorney General, I am mindful of the provisions of Section 3 of the Twenty-fifth Amendment to the Constitution and of the uncertainties of its application to such brief and temporary periods of incapacity. I do not believe that the drafters of this amendment intended its application to situations such as the instant one.
>
> Nevertheless, consistent with my longstanding arrangement with Vice President George Bush, and not intending to set a precedent binding anyone privileged to hold the office in the future, I have determined and it is my intention and direction, that Vice President George Bush shall discharge those powers and duties in my stead commencing with the administration of anesthesia to me in this instance.
>
> I shall advise you and the Vice President when I determine that I am able to resume the discharge of the constitutional powers and duties of this office.
>
> May God bless this nation and us all.
>
> > Sincerely,
> > Ronald Reagan

T. Burton Smith M.D., personal physician to President Reagan, in the White House Medical Office consultation room. This office, with its two treatment rooms, has been used to care for the past seven presidents. It is located on the ground floor of the White House.

Vice President George Bush, my other patient, was warm and friendly during our meetings at the White House or at his home.

President Reagan enjoyed discussing horsemanship with his agents and me before saddling-up El Alamain for his morning ride at the ranch.

The president was relaxed and happy when working on his ranch in California, driving his Jeep, and accompanied by his dogs.

Since I had to be near President Reagan at all times, I helped clear brush at the Reagan ranch in California.

The South Lawn is a scene of exciting military pageantry upon the arrival of a dignitary for a State visit.

Awaiting the start of a motion picture in the Reagan's living room at Camp David.

The First Family depart the heliport for an annual examination at Bethesda Naval Hospital. Commander Dunn with the "football," Dr. Smith, Dr. Hutton, Rex, and the Reagans.

The security and privacy of Camp David allowed the Reagans the freedom of going for daily walks.

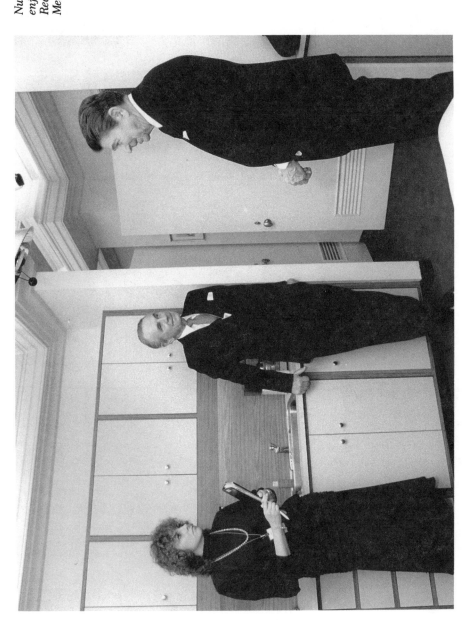

Nurse Dianne Capps and I enjoy a visit by President Reagan to the White House Medical Office.

The entrance to Camp David decorated for the holiday season.

The Reagans made
Christmas in the
White House very
special. The senior
staff reception
included a
Christmas greeting
and photograph in
front of the White
House Christmas
tree.

Christmas at the White House 1986. The entire Smith family was able to enjoy the decorations and the White House Christmas tree in the Blue Room.

The president and Mrs. Reagan wave New Year's greetings to the guests at El Dorado Country Club in Palm Desert, California enroute to a private dinner party.

A fun moment upon receiving a good report during a post-operative visit to the hospital.

The Commander-in-Chief departs the Bethesda Naval Hospital to the warm applause of the hospital staff. President Reagan looked and felt fit on the seventh post-operative day following major abdominal surgery in July 1985.

The "President's Men" depart the diplomatic entrance to board the presidential helicopter enroute to an event. L-R: the White House Press; Larry Speaks (presidential spokesman); Donald Regan (Chief-of-Staff to the president); Jim Kuhn (assistant to the president); President Reagan and Dr. Smith in the rear. May 30, 1985.

President Reagan enjoyed talking to the staff members aboard Air Force One. July 1985.

Dr. Smith with the personal physician to Secretary Mikhail Gorbachev at the Maison De Saussure during the first Summit meeting in Geneva, Switzerland November 19, 1985.

A warm cordial greeting from the Gorbachevs during the Geneva Summit, November 20, 1985.

During the Geneva Summit, our hosts at the Russian Mission, supplied the staff with vodka and caviar but no spoons. I solved the problem by supplying wooden tongue blades. L-R: William Henkel (director of advance); Jim Kuhn, Dr. Smith, Commander Patrick Dunn, and Grey Terry (advance).

Perhaps one of the most historical moments of the Reagan Administration was the walk from the formal US-Russian Summit meeting at Villa Fleur D'eau to the informal fireside talk in the poolhouse on the first day of the Geneva Summit, November 17, 1985.

Dear Kit & Burton – Thanks for so many things &
Very Best Wishes & Regards.
Ronald Reagan

*A departure photograph
taken with President Reagan
in the Oval Office reception
room.*

Vice President Bush was up in his vacation home in Kennebunkport, Maine, and when we realized we would have to perform open surgery on the president we asked him to return to Washington and stand by. He flew back to town on Saturday, went directly to his official residence at the U.S. Naval Observatory, and said he would sit on the veranda waiting for something to happen.

Keeping the First Lady Posted

The president had been given a sedative in his suite and was drowsy as he was wheeled along on a gurney from the old building, across a ramp to the new building, and on toward the operating room with Mrs. Reagan again walking beside him holding his hand. She said her good-byes to him outside the operating room door, and at 11 A.M. returned to the sitting room in the presidential suite where I promised to keep her posted by telephone on the progress of the operation. I called her when the president's powers were supposed to have been turned over to Vice President Bush following the administration of the anesthetic, and again a few minutes later at 11:28 A.M. when Dr. Oller made his first incision.

The operating room was fairly small and painted off-white, with powerful overhead lights shining down on the operating table. The president was lifted from the gurney to the operating table, rolled on his side by the anesthesiologist and his assistant, and given a spinal-type anesthesia which numbed the lower part of his body. The anesthesiologist and his assistant then disappeared behind a sterile curtain at the head of the operating table where they monitored instruments measuring the president's blood pressure, pulse, heart, breathing, and other vital signs throughout the operation.

Four surgeons led by Dr. Oller and assisted by three nurses gathered around the site of the president's operation visible through the sterile drapes covering his abdomen. The site was prepared for surgery, and a sedative was dripped into a vein in his right arm which put him to sleep in a few seconds.

Dr. Rosenberg, Ray Shaddick, and I stood behind the operating team on a raised platform so we could observe what was going on. I remember turning to Shaddick and saying, "Ray, you're certainly getting a great medical education," as he always seemed to be there when we were either examining the president or operating on him. I also remember thinking that here was the most important person in the world, which meant this operating room was probably the most important place on earth at that moment with history clearly in the making.

The operation Dr. Oller was about to perform on the president required only a good head and a good hand rather than an army of specialists and loads of exotic equipment. Sometimes surgeons will arrive at a point in an unusual operation where there are several ways to go, and in these cases they might stop and have a conference, or even call other people in. But this one was straightforward.

Dr. Oller made a long incision down the middle of President Reagan's abdomen and exposed the intestinal tract. The beginning of the large bowel containing the big polyp was identified, and the small intestine leading into it was divided. Then a second division was made in the large colon about two feet from the beginning, and the entire intestinal section containing the large polyp and two incidental small ones was gently and carefully removed to avoid spreading any tumor cells. Dr. Oller then sutured the two ends of the intestine back together again, and anticipated no problems from the removal of this fairly small section since the colon is quite long. The entire section of the colon which had been removed was very carefully lifted out so no cancerous tumor cells would come loose and spread to other parts of the president's body through his bloodstream. This section was immediately sent to the hospital's pathologist to determine the presence or absence of malignancy, and to see if any of the tumor had spread outside of the intestinal tract.

I called Mrs. Reagan and told her everything had gone well, and that I'd be accompanying the president to the recovery room and would meet her there. I had stayed near the president throughout the entire operation. I felt the military aide with the "football" was a bit superfluous at this point since the president was under anesthesia, or groggily coming out of it for some six hours. He was thus incapable of using the "football" to order a counterstrike against the Soviet Union had it attacked us with nuclear weapons. Whether another aide with a "football" was with the vice president, who was acting as president for these few hours, or whether the one with us would have rushed over to him in the event of an emergency, I do not know.

The operation lasted two hours and fifty-three minutes, and when it was over a dressing was put on the president's incision, he was lifted onto a gurney, and wheeled into the cavernous recovery room across the hall. There would normally have been a dozen or so patients on gurneys watched over by recovery room nurses. But on this occasion the president was the only patient there. It was eerie.

Mrs. Reagan came in with her stepbrother, Dr. Richard Davis, who was a neurosurgeon like his late father, Dr. Loyal Davis, and had driven down from his home in Philadelphia to be with her. He was very supportive as they stood by the president's bed, and Mrs. Reagan held her husband's hand as he slept. The two of them would leave the president's side and return to the sitting room in the presidential suite for awhile, and then come back again as he gradually came out of the anesthetic. President Reagan was receiving normal postoperative antibiotics through an intravenous drip, and was hooked up to machines monitoring his vital signs which, among other things, enabled us to see a tracing of the electrical impulses powering his heart.

I stayed with the president in the recovery room, while the other six doctors who had been with me in the operating room went off to hold a press conference. There was some criticism that I should have been at the press conference introducing everybody and describing the operation. But I felt my job was to be with the president because if something happened while I was away at the press conference it would have been a little hard to explain.

Doctors often ask patients who are recovering from anesthesia a series of questions to see if its effects have worn off. The normal litany is: "What's your name? What hospital are you in? What's your room number? What's your address at home? And who's the president of the United States?" I never asked Ronald Reagan these questions because I knew that when I got to "Who's the President of the United States?" he'd look at me with a twinkle in his eye and say, "George Washington" or "Abe Lincoln."

Meeting the Press

Dr. Oller told the army of reporters the president was "doing beautifully," and that there was no visual evidence of cancer in the area surrounding the polyp. Dr. Oller was then asked how serious a threat it would be to the president's health if the polyp was found to be cancerous. He said such a cancer would probably be what's known as a "Dukes A" lesion in which the malignancy has not penetrated the wall of the colon, and from which there's "probably better than a 95 percent five-year survival rate."

It was at this point, about halfway through the press conference, that Dr. Steven Rosenberg, who had merely observed the operation from a distance, stepped in front of the microphone and took over the press conference. Dr. Rosenberg said there was only a 50-50 chance the president would survive his cancer during the next five years (even though we had not even begun the pathological examination of his malignancy to find out how serious it was). We quickly realized Dr. Rosenberg was much too visible, and his statements about President Reagan's condition much too premature, so we turned him off.

Mrs. Reagan would have loved to turn off media coverage of her husband's operation, which was all over television and in print. *Time* magazine had a color picture of the colonoscope going up the president's colon. And it seemed every TV station in the nation had invited a local doctor in to describe the president's operation assisted by graphic drawings of his insides. As the Reagans watched from his hospital suite, one TV doctor even volunteered that in his opinion the president had only four years or so to live. I asked the president if these lurid descriptions of his surgery bothered him and he said, "No, not if it helps somebody." But the First Lady thought otherwise.

The president rested in the recovery room for about five hours following his surgery, and a little after 7 P.M., Fred Fielding handed him a sheet of paper with two sentences on it which, when signed, would give him back his power as president and commander in chief. Fielding said the president had trouble reading the letter and that he thought it might be too soon to ask him to sign it since he seemed to be a little woozy. Fielding felt the worst thing in the world would be to have Ronald Reagan take back his power from Vice President Bush, and then have to transfer it back again because he wasn't yet alert enough to handle his job. The problem was that the president didn't have his contact lenses in, or his glasses on. This was remedied, and the president was asked if he understood the words. He replied, "Gimme a pen," and at 7:29 P.M. he resumed his duties as president of the United States. The letters to Messrs. Thurmond and O'Neill read:

> Following up on my letter to you of this date, please be advised I am able to resume the discharge of the constitutional powers and duties of the office of the President of the United States. I have informed the Vice President of my determination and my resumption of those powers and duties.

Mr. Reagan was returned to the presidential suite later that evening, and was plainly uncomfortable because of a tube we had put through his nose into his stomach. He wanted the tube taken out, but I had to say no. I told him it was there to get rid of gas in his intestinal tract which could stretch that little suture line holding his colon together. If that should happen, a leak might develop allowing possibly infectious material to seep into his abdomen, which could cause an abscess, forcing us to operate on him again. The president reminded me that no one had shoved a tube down his brother Neil's nose after he had the same operation only a few days earlier, and wanted to know why he was any different. I said because he was the president of the United States and his brother wasn't. I'm also sure the president didn't want any complications to occur and neither did we.

The First Lady arrived from the White House at about 10 A.M. on Sunday morning, July 14, and created a terrific photo opportunity by giving the president a big kiss while making sure her face covered the tube sticking out of his nose. The picture was snapped by a White House photographer, and copies were distributed to the press, who rushed it into print.

The president, despite his obvious discomfort, sat up in bed for about forty-five minutes, took a walk around his room, read a western novel, and watched television with Mrs. Reagan. She returned to the White House late in the afternoon, leaving me with her husband, who wanted to get out of there and go home.

The Polyp Was Cancerous

The next day, Monday, July 15, we received the results of the biopsy of the polyp we had removed forty-eight hours earlier. The news was not good. A four-column headline in the *New York Times* read: "Reagan's Doctors Find Cancer in Tumor But Report Removal Leaves His Chances Excellent." What the detailed examination showed was that the president's polyp was a "Dukes B" lesion in which the cancer has penetrated through the bowel wall into the muscle beneath it, instead of the less serious "Dukes A" variety where it's confined to the bowel wall itself. The survival rate for a "Dukes B" lesion is about 50 to 80 percent because of the possibility that the cancer will become a "Dukes C" lesion by breaking through the muscle wall into the lymph nodes from where it could spread throughout the body, reducing the victim's five-year survival rate to 37 percent.

A nationwide study of 1,300 patients done by the National Cancer Institute on October 1, 1989, showed that the drug levamisole in combination with another drug called 5-fluorouracil could raise the five-year survival rate for "Dukes C" cancer from 37 to 49 percent. This is very encouraging, and again illustrates the continuing advance of medical science. The Dukes system for identifying the severity of this kind of intestinal cancer, by the way, is named after Dr. Cuthbert E. Dukes, the British pathologist who devised it in 1932.

Dr. Oller, Dr. Hutton, Dr. Rosenberg, and I gave Mrs. Reagan a detailed report on her husband's cancer during a half-hour meeting with her in the sitting room of the presidential suite. She said, "We must tell the president about this," so the five of us filed into his room, and gathered around his bed while Dr. Oller, who had performed the surgery, told him the big polyp we had removed was cancerous.

President Reagan received the news about his cancer quite calmly and asked Dr. Oller if he had removed it all. Dr. Oller said he had, and the president said, "Well, that's that." As far as the president was concerned his cancer was gone and he could get on with his life. I wish more patients had this attitude, because it would certainly help speed their recovery.

The president continued his recovery the next day by meeting with Chief of Staff Don Regan for twenty-five minutes, walking up and down the hall with Mrs. Reagan, reading a biography of President Calvin Coolidge, and that evening watching Lauren Bacall and Humphrey Bogart in *To Have and Have Not*.

On the following day, July 17, the president was removed from intravenous feeding and put on a liquid diet. He also had his first postoperative meeting with Vice President George Bush. The First Lady had opposed an earlier meeting because she felt it would have unduly tired her husband, and I believe she was right.

Thursday, July 18, was a great day for the president, who joined Mrs. Reagan in waving at press photographers gathered below his third-floor hospital window, and had his first real meal of baked chicken and rice.

This was also the day when the *New York Times* carried a front-page story under a two-column headline saying that Navy captain Dr. Walter W. Karney, the internist who coordinated President Reagan's physical examinations at Bethesda during Dr. Ruge's tenure in 1984, and mine on March 8, 1985, had criticized my surgical team for waiting four months after finding a small polyp in the president's lower colon to do the colonoscopy that uncovered a far larger one.

I had discussed all this with Dr. Cattau in March 1985, and in his written report to me he stated that there was no urgency about removing the small benign polyp. So it wasn't until the president returned from the Bonn economic summit that we decided to remove it, which was fine with Dr. Cattau. After the small polyp was removed, and while the president was still prepared and sedated, I said it seemed a perfect opportunity to evaluate the remainder of his colon, which was fortunate since we came upon the much bigger polyp. My reaction to Dr. Karney's comment is that we followed accepted medical practices on March 8, and again on July 12 when I decided to go the extra mile and we found the big polyp. Hindsight, I have found during a lifetime in medicine, is always a good deal easier than foresight.

President Reagan's recovery continued on Friday, July 19, with the welcome news that he could go home the next day, topped off with a gourmet dinner of pink salmon, fresh corn, fruit slaw, and peach melba.

The president did his regular five-minute weekly radio broadcast on Saturday, July 20, and then he and the First Lady helicoptered back to the White House, where they were greeted by balloons, "Welcome Home" signs, and 2,000 administration officials and their families. A Marine Corps jazz band played "When the Saints Go Marching In" as the president and First Lady strolled into the White House through the Diplomatic Entrance, took the elevator up to their residence, and walked out on the Truman balcony to greet everyone and wave. I went directly to my medical office in the on the first floor next to the Diplomatic Entrance.

Chapter Nine

Exploring the Transfer of Presidential Power

Two days after we returned to the White House following President Reagan's surgery, I received a note from his White House spokesman, Larry Speakes, thanking me for helping him understand what Ronald Reagan had just gone through so he could brief reporters. The note read:

Dear Dr. Smith:

Let me say how much I appreciate your providing me with solid background during the President's illness.

Your willingness to share with me information enabled me to move through the minefield of press questions with some semblance of knowing what I was talking about.

Again, many thanks.

Best regards,
Larry

Mark Weinberg, Larry's assistant, also sent me a note saying: "You were a key part of our effort to inform and reassure the public and I appreciate everything you did to help us."

These notes pleased me because I wanted the American people to have an accurate picture of their president's health. They also helped heal my working relationship with Larry and Mark, which had been badly damaged following the candid briefing I had given them on President Reagan's physical examination four months earlier. It was this briefing that resulted in the First Lady's requesting me to always brief her about her husband's medical condition first, "and then *we* talk to Larry," since the family should be notified first.

Welcoming China's President Li Xiannian

Shortly before the president left for the Bethesda Naval Medical Center, I received a memorandum from Bunny Murdock, the State Department's assistant chief of protocol for visits, giving me some background on the forthcoming state visit of the People's Republic of China's President Li Xiannian, which had her worried. The memo noted that:

> President Li is reportedly 76 years old although some sources say that he is quite a bit older than that. He has some back problems but we are unsure as to his health in general.
> The Chinese have been very careful not to schedule him for more than any two hour period. They are very worried about the State Dinner and the length of time. I am worried about the arrival ceremony and the heat.
> He always travels with two doctors and two nurses in attendance. I will attach their names.
> Of course the Secret Service will know the closest hospitals etc. . . . but I thought that I should alert you also to be on the safe side. With any luck I hope not to be calling you and your staff!!

On Tuesday, July 23, three days after President Reagan arrived back at the White House from Bethesda, and while still recovering from major surgery, he greeted President Li Xiannian as he arrived at the White House for a 10:30 A.M. meeting in the Oval Office.

The president walked over to Mr. Li's limousine, welcomed his obviously feeble guest, who was dressed in a Mao suit and dark glasses. In his usual gracious way the president helped Mr. Li out of his car, out of his chair after their meeting in the Oval Office, and continued to physically assist his elderly guest in every way he could.

This worried me because President Reagan had been on the operating table just ten days earlier, and I had recommended that he have no physical exertion for six weeks. The sutures holding his incision together could be weakening, yet his body had only begun its healing process. You might say that the "glue" which was keeping the president in one piece was not quite dry, and any exertion might have pulled his sutures apart, forcing me to put him back in the hospital for repairs.

President Li attended a White House state dinner held in his honor, but left after the formal toasts following dinner without enjoying the evening's entertainment provided by Metropolitan Opera soprano Grace Bumbry and baritone Gregg Baker. I insisted the president leave as well, and accompanied him up in the elevator to his residence along with Ray Shaddick, who stationed himself outside the residence door. When I saw there was nobody there to help the president, I became his valet as well as his doctor. I stood outside his bathroom door as he handed me his clothes which I hung up for him. He put on his pajamas, and I helped him crawl gingerly into bed. I looked over his incision to make sure everything was in order, chatted with him for a while, and told him I'd be right upstairs if he needed me.

Sleeping in the White House

I wanted to keep a close eye on President Reagan for the next few days and thought about sleeping on the rollout bed in my White House office. But I believe it was the First Lady who suggested I stay in one of the five guest suites on the third floor of the White House directly above the president's bedroom, which I did. It was quite a pleasant experience. Every morning I'd order breakfast of toast, whole grain cereal, and coffee, and a White House usher would serve it to me along with the *Washington Post* in the sunlit, glass-enclosed solarium above the north portico, which President Reagan had used a lot when he was recovering from the Hinkley shooting. I'd examine the president in the morning, return to my office during the day, and check him over again at night, telling him I'd be right upstairs if he needed me.

Ronald Reagan's fast recovery from major surgery was helped by the fact that he was in outstanding physical shape for a man of seventy-four. He was proud of the way he looked, and worked at taking care of himself. When we did the CAT scan of his body, the young female radiologist who interpreted the results told the president he had the insides of a man half his age, which pleased him and Mrs. Reagan immensely.

The president has a wonderful sense of humor, which I'm sure also had a lot to do with his speedy recovery from his surgery. He was joking with us during his stay at Bethesda, just as he had with everyone at George Washington University Hospital four years earlier after he had been shot. When the First Lady came into his hospital room for the first time back then, he said, "Honey, I forgot to duck." When his surgeons arrived to remove the bullet he said, "I hope you're all Republicans." And when Treasury Secretary James Baker, III, and presidental counselor Edwin Meese came by to wish him well, he greeted them with, "Who's minding the store?"

Dealing with Skin Problems

I examined the president in the White House family quarters on July 30, two weeks after his operation, and noticed an abrasion on the right side of his nose, which was covered by a scab. The president figured it was caused by a piece of adhesive tape attached to that annoying tube I had put down his nose to prevent a buildup of gas in his intestinal tract. I had the scab removed from the president's nose using a local anesthetic injected underneath it. I then covered his nose with a small round bandage, and sent the scab to Bethesda's pathology lab for analysis. I said the sliver had been taken from Tracy Malone, a military nurse assigned to my White House medical unit.

I used a fictitious name because I've spent my entire medical life around hospitals, and I knew the speculation and conjecture that occurs when you send a lab a sample with the name of a well-known person such as Ronald Reagan on it. Somebody is always likely to say, "Hey, here's a sample of the president's blood," or "Here's a scab from the president's nose. Let's divide it up and sell the bits as souvenirs." The same thing applied to Ronald Reagan's early medical records on file at Saint John's Hospital in Santa Monica where I practiced. I knew some newspaper reporter might be tempted to pay a file clerk a handsome sum to copy them, so I had them sequestered when he was elected president.

On Thursday, August 1, President Reagan showed up with the small circular bandage on his nose as he spoke before a group of religious broadcasters in the White House. Reporters spotted it right away, and asked the president's spokesman, Larry Speakes, "What's that?" Larry said the skin on the president's nose had been aggravated by a piece of adhesive tape used to hold a tube in place in his nose when he was recovering from surgery a few days ago in the hospital. He said a tiny scab had formed and that it had been removed without the use of anesthetic. And, "no further treatment is necesary."

I was blindsided at about 8 P.M. that evening when I was alone in my office and received a call on my unlisted telephone. It was a reporter from the Associated Press, and to this day I don't know how he found my private number. Larry and Mrs. Reagan had been calling me all day about the biopsy flap, and when the phone rang I figured it was the First Lady with something else on her mind. Instead, it was the AP reporter asking me if it were true that the sore on the president's nose had been biopsied. I started to say, "No comment," but the guy hung up after the word "No" and immediately put an item out on the AP wire, which goes to almost all newspapers and radio and television stations in America, saying that Dr. Smith had confirmed that President Reagan had not had a biopsy to test for cancer.

On Saturday, August 3, while my wife, Kit, and I were at Camp David with the president and First Lady, a report was telephoned to me which said the scab on the president's nose was cancerous, but had nothing to do with his colon cancer. I walked right over to Aspen Lodge and told the president, who again took the news quite calmly.

President Reagan met in the Oval Office on Monday, August 5, with a small group of reporters and photographers, and when one of them questioned the Band-Aid on his nose, he said, "I thought you'd never ask." The president told the reporters he had a pimple and "squozed" it, and then admitted that a basal cell carcinoma had been found and removed.

This whole trivial matter of a spot on Ronald Reagan's nose had needlessly compromised the credibility of the president's chief White House spokesman and his personal physician. The president himself was not concerned, and ordered that medical information about his physical condition not be withheld from the press in the future.

What really amused me about this incident was that the East Coast press didn't seem to understand that we southern Californians get these precancerous sun lesions all the time. We're always out in the sun boating, playing tennis, gardening, jogging, and sunbathing, so they're extremely common. The First Lady had a spot removed from her lip. I had one removed from my nose. They're no big deal as long as you get rid of them in time. But prevention is still the best policy. A fact too many sun worshipers have learned to their sorrow who didn't catch their skin cancers until it was too late.

Resting at the Reagan Ranch

We went up to Camp David again that weekend, and then flew on to the Reagan ranch in California on August 11. Not much happens in Washington during the torrid days of August. Both the House and Senate are in recess.

President Reagan was invited to helicopter up to San Francisco, land on the deck of the aircraft carrier *Enterprise,* and give a talk on August 14 marking the fortieth anniversary of the end of the war with Japan. I knew the president's abdominal incision was not yet strong, and that this trip was not a good idea. So I talked with Don Regan and we enlisted the services of Vice President Bush to give the talk. General Douglas MacArthur's eighty-six-year-old widow was in the audience when Mr. Bush said that after the Japanese attacked Pearl Harbor, "We learned that when free people close their eyes to evil, they do so at their peril."

The president completed his recovery from colon cancer at the ranch by going for longer and longer walks, driving around in his old Jeep, later riding his horse, and finally by returning to Washington and resuming his normal activities from which he never looked back. That's why he'll tell you today that "I had cancer, but I don't have cancer now because it's been removed."

President Reagan's high-visibility bout with colon cancer has made the public aware of its dangers as never before. An article in the Spring 1989 issue of *Health Affairs* noted that the number of checkups for colon cancer had soared "in the latter half of 1985, presumably in response to the cancer detected by colonoscopy in President Reagan" and that these "rates continued to climb throughout 1986 [with] no indication they will return to pre-presidential levels."

President Reagan has spent more than his fair share of time in hospitals, and when he was under my care I'd always choose a military rather than a civilian one. Military hospitals are set up to handle the chaos surrounding a visit from the president of the United States. They can isolate the area the president will be staying in as we did at Bethesda, and they can guarantee his security.

Going Through Channels

After the discovery and treatment of the skin cancer on President Reagan's nose, the dermatologist who looked after him enlisted the president's help in declaring a "Skin Care Observation Week." I wanted him to declare a "Prostate Cancer Observation Week" too because prostate cancer is far more deadly than skin cancer. The prostate gland is a walnut-size gland situated at the base of the urinary bladder, and it secretes a milky fluid that makes up part of the male semen. Prostate cancer is the second most common form of cancer among men over fifty after lung cancer, and is responsible for 11 percent of all cancer deaths. Quite a few of the president's friends have cancer of the prostate. A lot of my friends have it. Two justices of the Supreme Court had it. And if you wait until symptoms develop, the cat's out of the bag, although in many cases it can be controlled.

What I hadn't realized was that to get a special week of any kind declared you must enlist fifty members of Congress to sponsor it. So I called U.S. Senator Pete Wilson, from my home state of California, and said this was what I wanted to do. I had become acquainted with Wilson during a trip he took on Air Force One when he was recovering from an appendectomy, and I had offered to help if he had any problems. Wilson, who has since been elected governor of California, got back to me and said there was no official "Prostate Cancer Observation Week," and that even though he thought it was a good idea, his staff just didn't have time to do all the legwork needed to get fifty members of Congress to push the idea. So I said, "What if the president wants it done?" "Oh, well that's different," he said, "because then it would be done."

So I went directly to the president, but without using the unique personal access I had to him. Instead, I wrote him a letter suggesting that he declare a "Prostate Cancer Observation Week," and asked his executive assistant Jim Kuhn to see that he received it. A mountain of mail addressed to the president arrives at the White House every day, and if I had gone through regular channels the president would probably never have seen my letter. This is so even though almost all correspondence addressed to the president is answered by the staff. I believe, however, there's some kind of code you can put on the envelope so the letter will be delivered directly to the president without being opened. Whether or not the president ever read my letter I don't know. What I do know is that he never mentioned anything to me about it, nor did he ever declare a "Prostate Cancer Observation Week." This was a great disappointment to me because I feel it's terribly important to alert American men to the threat of prostate cancer and the need for regular checkups.

A timely example of a breakthrough in medicine is the isolation, purification, and measurement of a circulating substance unique to prostate tissue: prostatic-specific antigen (PSA).

Normally, the level in the bloodstream is low, rises modestly due to benign enlargement, and reaches higher levels when prostate cancer is present. Thus, using a drawn blood sample, it would seem that it would be ideal for screening large populations of men to detect early cancer of the prostate. Early cancer of the prostate commonly has no symptoms and it is during this period of growth that it can be surgically cured. Large-group testing has been carried out in many centers, over the past few years, to better define the results and its application.

Several exciting uses of PSA are becoming apparent. Higher levels may be useful in determining if the tumor is confined to the prostate gland or has spread beyond, thus limiting the usefulness of surgery. Rising PSA levels following radiation therapy are a valuable marker but may be a bad sign. More investigation is required to evaluate this area. Monitoring the PSA level following surgery or other forms of treatment is an indispensable guide to success or failure of the therapy.

The need to let the public know that such a test exists, how to make it affordable, and how to interpret the results will do a great deal to reduce the awesome rise in occurrence of this common disease.

Transferring Presidential Power

While the president's operation for a cancerous polyp is now history and his periodic checkups normal, lively debate continues over exactly what events should trigger the transfer of power from president to vice president under the Twenty-fifth Amendment to the Constitution. The pressure to pass this amendment was generated by the fear of a constitutional crisis following the assassination of President John F. Kennedy on November 22, 1963, and it was ratified a little over three years later on February 10, 1967.

Dr. Ruge, who preceded me as President Reagan's White House physician, and whom I've had a chance to talk to at his home in Denver, Colorado, since I left Washington, believes power should have been temporarily transferred to Vice President Bush after President Reagan was shot by John W. Hinkley, Jr.

Dr. Ruge says he carried a copy of the Twenty-fifth Amendment in his medical bag, but had not thought about it during all the excitement at the George Washington University Hospital, where President Reagan was rushed for emergency chest surgery to remove the bullet lodged in his left lung. Dr. Ruge believes this was the ideal time to use it because of the seriousness of President Reagan's wound, and says the president was perfectly able to sign a letter temporarily turning his power over to Vice President Bush right up until the moment he went under anesthesia.

Dr. Ruge went on to say that Vice President Bush asked him to brief the cabinet on the president's condition at 7:30 A.M. on the morning after his surgery, during which he received quite a bit of blood to replace blood he had lost, thus reducing the effects of shock. Dr. Ruge said no one at that meeting asked him if Mr. Reagan was well enough to function as president, probably because of the way he joked with visitors in his hospital room and was seemingly his old self. Dr. Ruge still feels he should have raised the question of transferring power from the president to the vice president via the Twenty-fifth Amendment, and regrets he didn't do it.

A report called "A Heartbeat Away," recently issued by a study group that included former White House aides brought together by the Twentieth Century Fund, said the temporary transfer of power from the president to the vice president should be more routine and not seen as a sign of presidential weakness. In a newspaper interview shortly before he became president, George Bush said he had not discussed the Twenty-fifth Amendment with his running mate, Dan Quayle, because it never occurred to him to do so.

President Bush and Vice President Quayle are well-informed about the Twenty-fifth Amendment today, in part because of a meeting held in the White House Oval Office on the morning of April 18, 1989. The meeting was arranged by the president's personal physician, Dr. Burton Lee, and included Presidential Counsel Boyden Gray, Chief of Staff John Sununu, and the head of the Secret Service.

Dr. Lee had prepared for the Oval Office meeting by reviewing the conclusions of a symposium held at the University of Virginia's White Burkett Miller Center of Public Affairs on September 30, 1986. The symposium had been called to discuss the findings of the center's Commission on Presidential Disability and the Twenty-fifth Amendment, which had begun its work back in 1985 when I became President Reagan's White House physician. The commission was chaired by the two men who fathered the Twenty-fifth Amendment: Herbert Brownell, attorney general in the Eisenhower Administration, and Birch Bayh, former U.S. senator from Indiana, who were assisted by a small group of other distinguished experts in the field including former chief justice of the Supreme Court Warren E. Burger.

I met in August 1989 with some of the people who had participated in the work of the commission, when I was cornered by a psychiatrist who challenged me at considerable length because I had never done a basic intelligence test on President Reagan. He said I should have done one, and then compared its results with one done a year later to see if he was failing mentally. I said I did this by simply observing the president's day-to-day behavior. But my psychiatrist colleague said that was not enough because it didn't indicate with any kind of precision whether his mental capacity is better, worse, or the same a year later. He wanted me to do tests on the president such as having him subtract nines from one hundred until he got to zero—100, 91, 82, 73, etc. My reaction was, what to do if he gets his nines right this year, but goofs next year? Do you tell him to pack his things and go home to California?

In its own way, this talk with the psychiatrist was a good introduction to the heart of the symposium, which was the Miller Center's thirty-two-page report that looked at the Twenty-fifth Amendment's four major sections (only the last of which considers the murky area of interest to the psychiatrist).

The report recalled that "Eight of the 35 men who have occupied the White House have died in office, four of them victims of assassins. Several have had serious illnesses, some of which at the time were hidden from those who should have been told, as well as from the public."

The report goes on to say that while Sections 1 and 2 of the Twenty-fifth Amendment have already been used and presented no serious problems, Sections 3 and 4 could cause trouble and are therefore considered in some detail.

Section 1 of the Twenty-fifth Amendment simply says that if the president is removed from office, or dies, the vice president shall become president. This section has worked perfectly since Vice President John Taylor succeeded to the nation's highest office following the death of President William Henry Harrison in 1841.

Section 2 deals with what should be done when a president is removed from office, or dies, and there is no sitting vice president, as occurred most recently in 1974 when President Richard Nixon resigned, and Vice President Gerald Ford became president, leaving the office of vice president vacant. (It was filled when President Ford nominated former New York governor Nelson A. Rockefeller, a non-elected official who conceivably might have become president. He was confirmed by the Senate 121 days later.)

Section 3 of the Twenty-fifth Amendment is the one President Reagan was "mindful of," but did not believe was meant to apply to situations like his in which he was being put to sleep for only a few hours to have a polyp removed. Since the president is the only person who can or cannot invoke this section, what he says goes.

It's interesting to note that President George Bush saw things quite differently during the first week of May 1991, when he was bothered by an irregular heartbeat. It was felt he might have to undergo a general anesthetic while his doctors used an electric shock procedure to stop and then restart his heart, hoping it would resume its normal rhythm. President Bush was quite willing to sign an undated letter turning his powers over to Vice President Dan Quayle during the few minutes he'd be asleep. Fortunately, this procedure wasn't necessary, as the president's heart arrhythmia was successfully treated with medication.

Section 4 involves a sick president who refuses or is unable to confront his disability. It states that the vice president, and a majority of the president's cabinet (or some other body created by Congress) can decide to make the vice president the acting president by declaring in writing to the president pro tempore of the Senate and the Speaker of the House of Representatives "that the president is unable to discharge the powers and duties of his office."

The report believes that in retrospect, Section 4 could have applied to the final period of Woodrow Wilson's presidency, or of Franklin D. Roosevelt's. In a booklet called *Papers on Presidential Disability and the Twenty-fifth Amendment by Six Medical, Legal and Political Authorities,* assembled by the Miller Center, Dr. Kenneth R. Crispell, one of the six authorities, talks about the illness of Wilson and FDR, and how they remained in office even though they were both obviously far too ill to govern. Dr. Crispell says Mrs. Woodrow Wilson "ran the government" of the United States for eighteen months with the help of Senator Carter Glass and the physician to the president, Admiral Cary T. Grayson, and that President Roosevelt was so desperately ill that he was admitted to the Bethesda Naval Medical Center twenty-eight times under assumed names from early 1943 to early 1944. Crispell goes on to note that Roosevelt was only able to sit up for about two hours a day during the historic Yalta conference with Churchill and Stalin, which ended two months before he died on April 12, 1945.

Dr. Burton Lee spent a substantial part of April 7 and 8, 1989, reviewing the commission's report with those involved with it, and asked that fifteen copies be rushed to him for his meeting in the president's Oval Office.

I understand the meeting went well and that a good deal of time was devoted to the question of catastrophic illness and the importance of following the provisions of the Twenty-fifth Amendment. It was felt that if the president is unable to sign the papers turning his powers over to the vice president under Section 3 of the amendment, then the provisions of Section 4 should be followed so that the vice president, members of the cabinet, or the Congress can effect the transfer. An action on principles was also established whereby if the president "goes down," his physician will call the chief of staff, who will notify the vice president and the president's counsel so that a discussion about the transfer of presidential power can begin. This procedure was scheduled to be tested at Camp David.

What all this says to me is that the Rubicon has at last been crossed on presidential disability, and that it will be handled much more expeditiously in the future than it has in the past. This will benefit the nation and the world by ensuring the orderly transfer of power in the United States of America.

Chapter Ten

Inside Camp David and the Reagan Ranch

President Reagan always liked to say that "the work never changes, only the scenery." And some of the scenery he enjoyed most was at Camp David in Maryland's Catoctin Mountains, some seventy miles from Washington, D.C., or about half an hour away by helicopter. The president enjoyed Camp David's wooded terrain, which is totally secured by Marine Corps troops guarding the perimeter, and the Secret Service, which protects those inside. This allows the president, the First Lady, and their guests to stroll around Camp David's many asphalt and wilderness trails seemingly unescorted even though they are constantly observed by unobtrusive armed guards. Security is tightened still further by prohibiting picture taking anywhere but inside the various lodges and other buildings. The whole place is maintained by a construction battalion of U.S. Navy Seabees: carpenters, plumbers, electricians, and others, with bachelors living in a barracks on site and married men housed outside with their families.

The Genesis of Camp David

Camp David was built in 1942 as a retreat for President Franklin D. Roosevelt, who could no longer enjoy his favorite pastimes of deep-sea fishing in the Atlantic Ocean, then infested with Nazi U-boats, or time-consuming train trips away from the White House to bathe in the mineral-rich waters of Warm Springs, Georgia, which he felt strengthened his crippled legs. FDR's new getaway was secure, close to Washington, and a welcome relief from the capital's oppressive summertime heat. Now all it needed was a name, and it came to the president following General Jimmy Doolittle's daring B-25 raid on Tokyo, launched from the aircraft carrier *Hornet* steaming through the Pacific Ocean six hundred miles away. When mystified reporters asked the president where the raid had originated, he said it came from Shangri-La (site of the isolated Tibetan monastery described in James Hilton's novel *Lost Horizon*). President Dwight D. Eisenhower renamed the place Camp David after his grandson David Eisenhower, and over the years it has been used by eight presidents and some two dozen distinguished foreign visitors, including British Prime Minister Winston Churchill, Soviet General Secretary Brezhnev, and, most recently, Prime Minister John Major.

A cordial meeting between President Eisenhower and Soviet Premier Nikita Khrushchev produced the familiar phrase, "Spirit of Camp David," which reappeared years later following the peace accord that President Jimmy Carter negotiated there between Egypt's President Anwar as-Sadat and Israel's Prime Minister Menachem Begin. It took President Carter thirteen days of whirlwind diplomacy, including endless walks between Sadat's cabin and Begin's, before the two leaders were willing to sign the Camp David Accords on behalf of their countries, which had been bitter enemies for years.

President Reagan's staff always accompanied him on weekend trips to Camp David. Accompanying him were his executive assistant, Jim Kuhn, constantly on the telephone to the White House relaying messages to and from the president; Assistant Press Secretary Mark Weinberg, who dealt with the media; the military aide responsible for communications and the "football"; and me, his personal physician. We staff people were allowed to bring our families with us since our jobs required us to spend so much time away from home. It was wonderful having my wife, Kit, with me, and the chance to walk, jog, bird-watch, study the variety of eastern shrubs and trees, and play tennis on Camp David's two well-maintained clay courts.

We staffers spent a great deal of time at Laurel Lodge, which, like all the other main buildings, is of wooden construction and painted moss green. Local fieldstone was used for the outside trim and chimney, and there are large picture windows bringing in both light and views of the surrounding woods. President Reagan had a large conference room with a massive wooden boardroom meeting table, and the flags of the fifty states plus his personal presidential flag lining the walls of the room.

The staff loved Laurel Lodge, which has a spacious and comfortably rustic living room, recreation rooms, television, VCR with cassettes ranging from classics to children's films for the kids of staffers, and a revolving list of twenty feature films we adults could have projected at any one of several locations. A full-size popcorn machine was kept going at top speed whenever movies were being shown, and we saw so many that at one point I suggested we have our own version of Academy Awards night.

We ate our meals in Laurel Lodge's dining room, served by Navy mess stewards who were mostly from the Philippines and treated us to everything from outdoor barbecues when the weather was warm and sunny to ethnic dishes garnished with raw vegetables artistically arranged to resemble flowers. Kit frequently played housemother to Jim and Carole Kuhn's children, and was always available when the Marine helicopter pilots wanted to talk about their families while passing around treasured photographs. These young men spent most of their on-duty hours testing and polishing the president's helicopter undoubtedly making it the most well-maintained chopper on earth.

A few steps away from Laurel Lodge is Holly Lodge, which is a smaller recreational complex mainly used by the staff, although past presidents would often bring foreign leaders there after dinner to sit and talk on its very pleasant front porch. Holly Lodge has a library, attractive reading room, billiard table, motion picture room, and an "honor" bar we rarely used because we were always on call, never knew when we might be needed, and certainly didn't want to leave a paper trail of bar chits behind if our performance was ever called into question. Every two weeks or so we would get a bill for the meals we ate at Laurel Lodge and anything we drank at Holly Lodge.

Camp David is spread out over several hundred heavily wooded acres. You can get snowed in during the wintertime, making it impossible to rush the president to a hospital by helicopter. It's even pretty hairy trying to get an ambulance down the icy, fog-covered mountain roads to nearby Hagerstown Hospital when you're not snowed in, not to mention the communications "dead spots" which occur in this kind of weather, making it impossible to alert the hospital staff that the president of the United States was being rushed there for treatment. I didn't like to go to Camp David during the winter even though the sparkling snow and trees hung with icicles made it incredibly beautiful. I felt medically isolated up there; but it was my job, so I did it.

Camp David itself is equipped to handle only minor medical emergencies. It has a sick bay (Navy parlance for a first-aid station), five Navy medical corpsmen on duty when the president is in residence, two Navy ambulances, and the president's HMX1 helicopter, housed in its own hangar. My mission was to be ready for any medical emergency. So I carefully inspected all these facilities, and drilled the medical unit so that we, assisted by the Secret Service, were prepared for anything: car or horse accidents, gunfire, shootouts with intruders, and whatever else we could think of. Fortunately, none of this contingency planning was ever put to the test. But we were ready if it had been.

The designated hospital for Camp David was the Naval Hospital in Bethesda about a half hour away. If I couldn't get the president there because of bad weather, I was ready to helicopter him to a secondary hospital only several minutes away in Hagerstown, Maryland, where the emergency room doctor was a fellow alumnus of mine from the University of Southern California.

The landing pad on the top of the hospital wasn't strong enough to withstand the heavy weight of the president's helicopter, so we'd have had to land in a nearby athletic field and transfer the president to an ambulance or station wagon for the dash to the hospital. If the weather were so bad we couldn't helicopter the president from Camp David to Hagerstown, I was ready to get him there by ambulance despite the problems mentioned earlier.

It looked like everything might be needed when President Jimmy Carter collapsed from heat exhaustion at Camp David as he started out on a ten-kilometer race that was being sponsored outside the grounds. Dr. William M. Lukash was jogging beside the president, who quickly recovered. The incident, however, was front-page news, and was featured on all the nightly TV news shows.

Weekend Relaxation

A nondenominational chapel, started by the Reagans, has been built at Camp David using private funds, and I'm sure a lot of people who work there, as well as the president and his family, would much prefer worshiping at Camp David than at a church miles away in town. The White House does not have a chapel, although worship services have been held there in the family theater normally used for meetings and movies.

The Reagans live in Aspen Lodge, which has a terraced rock garden sloping down to a swimming pool that they enjoyed during the hot summer weekends, but that was frozen solid during the winter. They treasured their absolute privacy, the lack of routine, and the chance to catch up on their reading of the latest issues of the *Washington Post, New York Times,* and *Los Angeles Times,* and the White House news summary and Louis L'Amour novels. President and Mrs. Reagan also looked forward to the horseback rides they took on Saturday afternoons and the long walks along Camp David's wilderness trails with their dog Lucky, who eventually became too strong to handle and was replaced by a little lapdog named Rex. Lucky's reward for years of faithful service was to be sent to the beautiful Reagan ranch in California to join three of their other dogs already in residence.

Since Camp David is a retreat, the Reagans rarely invited anyone to Camp David for the weekend except for family, close friends, and the British ambassador, Charles Price, who was a close friend and stayed in the VIP guest house right across from Aspen just before an official visit to Washington by his country's prime minister, Margaret Thatcher. I remember West German Chancellor Helmut Kohl and Japanese Premier Yasuhiro Nakasone lunching with President Reagan at Camp David, and how eager Mr. Nakasone and his party were to helicopter back to their embassy in Washington so they could watch a professional golf match which was on television that Saturday afternoon. All the meals at Aspen Lodge were prepared and served by the presidential watch made up of selected stewards and supervised by Eddie Serrano.

I'd helicopter to Camp David almost every weekend with the president and First Lady, and Kit would drive up in our Buick station wagon, arriving an hour or so later. The highlight of these weekends was the movies we'd watch with the Reagans every Friday and Saturday night. Kit and I would finish dinner with several other staff members in the main lodge, and then stroll over to meet the president and First Lady at Aspen Lodge.

There were usually about six of us waiting outside including the camp commander and the helicopter pilot, and a few seconds before 8:05 P.M., the president would walk out the door, we'd say, "Good evening, Mr. President," and he'd say, "Oh, come on in, we'll have a movie," as though he was surprised to see us out there.

On Friday we'd usually have what the president called "Golden Oldies" featuring John Wayne, Judy Garland, and other Hollywood stars, or occasionally himself in films such as *Hellcats of the Navy,* with Nancy Davis (later Nancy Reagan), and *King's Row* with Ann Sheridan. The president thought "King's Row" was one of his better films even though it was grisly and decidedly anti-doctor. In the film

Ronald Reagan goes out with a small town doctor's daughter, but the doctor doesn't like him, gets him into a hospital on some pretext or other, and cuts off his legs. When he wakes up he looks down at his amputated legs and says "Where's the rest of me?" which became the title of a book he wrote published in 1965. Another Ronald Reagan film is "Bedtime for Bonzo" in which he's teamed up with a monkey. The way to spot the monkey the president would say, was to look for the one who's not wearing a wristwatch.

On Saturday night we'd have the latest films such as the aerial combat thriller "Top Gun," or on one notorious evening "Kiss of the Spider Woman" which had been recommended by White House public relations man Mike Deaver who worked closely with the First Lady. This was a pretty sordid "R" rated movie which visibly embarrassed the Reagans. "This is not a very good way to spend an entertaining Saturday night," the president said, even though he and Mrs. Reagan saw it through to the bitter end.

The Reagans always sat on a sofa with bowls of popcorn and candy in front of them on a coffee table. Kit and I sat right behind them on two straight chairs, and every so often the president would take the bowl of popcorn in one hand and the candy in the other, lift them over his head, and let go so I'd have to catch them before they hit the floor, scattering candy and popcorn all over the place. The four or five other staff people sitting behind me hoped I'd miss. But I never did, thanks in part to Kit, who would always give me a nudge when she saw the two bowls headed my way.

As this was going on, White House chef Eddie Serrano would appear with soft drinks at exactly the halfway point of the movie. He served them while maneuvering around on his hands and knees so he wouldn't block the screen. The Reagans liked to bring their dog to the movies, and every time a horse, ballet dancer, or anything else in motion appeared, the dog would jump around and bark, bringing the show to a halt until he had regained his composure.

There was an unwritten rule that no one would talk until the movie was over. Then we'd all stand around, shifting from one foot to the other, and chat a bit with the president, who did most of the talking. The young Marine helicopter pilot and the camp commander were cautious and rarely said anything. But since I'd known the president for so long, and since I knew something about the movie business, I'd always have something to say, often in reply to a question from the president.

After the Judy Garland movie he asked if anyone knew how she died. Nobody did, so I went to the little library in Holly Lodge and found it was from an overdose of barbiturates in her London apartment at age forty-seven. After the John Wayne movie, he said, "You know, if I'd been around Hollywood a little longer I'd have probably made as many movies as John Wayne." And I said, "Well, how many did he make?" The president said, "I don't know, but I do know I made fifty-two or fifty-three." So I went over to the camp library again and found that John Wayne had made something like one hundred fifty movies, which I mentioned to the president the next time I saw him.

On one trip to Camp David the president looked down at a forest and said, " 'This is the forest primeval'—who wrote that?" I said I didn't know, but that I thought another part of it went, "Bearded with moss, and in garments green," and that Longfellow probably wrote it. The Holly Lodge library had a book of poems, and I looked it up. Sure enough, it was "Evangealine," by Henry Wadsworth Longfellow. So I called the president and said, "Mr. President, I've found it." And he said, "Good for you. I've been looking through our books here and it's bothered me. By the way," he added, "what were the trees in that poem?" I told him they were murmuring pines and hemlocks. Conversation with the First Lady was infrequent, formal, and revolved around dogs, flowers, the weather, and similar generalities.

On one of the helicopter rides back from Camp David to the White House, I noticed the president was reading Tom Clancy's best-selling thriller *Red Storm Rising,* possibly as part of his homework before a meeting with Soviet General Secretary Mikhail Gorbachev in Reykjavík, Iceland, only a few weeks away.

Rancho del Cielo

The president's ranch, which he helped build with his own hands, is named Rancho del Cielo (Ranch in the Sky). It's high enough up in the Santa Ynez Mountains so you can see the Pacific Ocean four or five miles away, where one of the most extraordinary events in naval history took place. I mention it because it's described in a book I gave the president for his seventy-fourth birthday. The book is called *Tragedy at Honda,* and it tells the story of "the greatest peacetime tragedy of the U.S. Navy," which occurred on September 8, 1923, when a squadron of fourteen destroyers was steaming down the California coast and became lost in a fog bank. The squadron's flagship made a wrong turn and headed directly toward Point Honda and an outcropping of ship-killing rocks, where it broke up and sank. Ten minutes later, obeying the unwritten follow-the-leader destroyer doctrine, nine more ships were impaled on the rocks, with seven going to the bottom.

I was familiar with this stretch of California coastline below the president's ranch because I was sent there as a young Naval doctor on February 24, 1942, after a Japanese minisubmarine had lobbed twenty-six shells into this area ten miles west of Santa Barbara. My job was to drive up and down this segment of coastline in a Jeep providing medical cover to a bunch of U.S. Coast Guard sailors patrolling the entire western shoreline from Canada to Mexico on foot, and to the crews of Navy blimps doing the same thing from overhead. I remember this assignment very well because it forced Kit and me to delay our wedding until the Japanese submarine scare died down and life returned to wartime normal.

It's about a seven-mile drive from the Pacific Coast Highway up a winding narrow road to the Reagans' 688-acre ranch and three-room adobe house built in 1872. The house has one bedroom and a large front porch where the president and First Lady ate many of their meals. The ranch was a perfect place for them to get away from it all until ABC, CBS, and NBC mounted giant telescopes on a nearby mountaintop so they could keep an ever-watchful eye on what the Reagans were doing down below.

The networks really couldn't see much because the whole area is well screened by tall trees. The Reagans knew this, and turned the tables on the prying eyes of the network TV cameramen by letting them see only what they wanted them to see. When President Reagan was recovering from his abdominal surgery, for example, he walked briskly through an open meadow so the TV crew could see how well he was recovering, and a little later he did the same thing on his horse. Mrs. Reagan, who has been leading the fight against drugs, rode her horse across the same meadow while holding up a sign reading "Just Say No!" An interesting twist occurred in this cat-and-mouse game when an enterprising independent cameraman with an unusually large telescopic lens began taking pictures of the Reagans and selling them to the networks, prompting all three to junk their costly spying operation.

It's rugged, isolated country up there. Tough to get in or out of when the fog rolls in, or during heavy rainstorms when rushing streams below the property flood the main road at several places. This presents no problem for all-terrain vehicles built high enough off the ground so they can ford the rushing streams with ease. But it can stop heavily armored presidential limousines in their tracks. I understand this happened when England's Queen Elizabeth and Prince Philip visited the ranch in 1983. They had to be transferred from their limousine to a rugged Land Rover.

The Reagan ranch is home to many wild animals, including mountain lions and poisonous snakes which can be seen among the wildflowers and oak trees. The president was so annoyed by all the snakes on the ranch that one day he and his helpers collected a slew of them, put them in grocery bags, and dumped them into a pond—now called "Snake Lake"—located beyond the edge of his property bordering on Los Padres National Forest. The Secret Service agents sitting outside guarding the ranch at night were worried about snakes, wildcats, and things jumping through the bushes at them even though they were armed and had infrared binoculars allowing them to spot intruders in the darkness.

I worried about the president's getting bitten by a rattlesnake because there are a lot of them in southern California, particularly up in the mountains, but the president wasn't afraid of them. He tells a story about how he once stomped on a rattler thinking he had his cowboy boots on when he was really wearing tennis shoes. So I naturally researched how I'd handle the president if he were hit by a rattler. I would have done all I could to slow the deadly venom from racing through his body and killing him. I might have immobilized his arm or leg, applied a tourniquet between the bite and his heart, put ice on to slow his circulation, and rushed him to the hospital, where they could monitor him to make sure he wasn't going into shock.

One thing I would not have done is given him antivenom serum, because fifty percent of the time a victim can overcome the effects of a bite without using antivenom, which carries risks of its own. A doctor friend, an orthopedist, was working in his garden and was bitten by a rattlesnake. He was given antivenom in the Santa Monica Hospital emergency room and subsequently went into shock, had a stroke, and has been paralyzed for many years now. There's no way of knowing whether it was a reaction to the snake bite, the antivenom, or the usual vascular causes involving an insufficient supply of blood to the tissues of the brain.

There's a guest house with two bedrooms and two baths on the ranch, where Queen Elizabeth and Prince Philip stayed when they visited, as did the president's children. President Reagan's daughter, Maureen, by his first wife, actress Jane Wyman (who was divorced in

1949), stayed there, as did their adopted son, Michael, and President and Mrs. Reagan's daughter, Patti, and son, Ron.

There was also a large trailer on the ranch, where I always stayed with the military aide toting the "football." Officers from the Army, Navy, Air Force, Marines, and Coast Guard were given this job for two years at a stretch, but they were rotated each weekend so they wouldn't have to spend too much time away from their regular duties. The Secret Service agents guarding the president also rotated, or "pushed," every eight hours. One agent would say to the other, "Who are you going to 'push' with today?" meaning who's taking your place when your eight-hour shift is up. No one seems to know the origin of this expression, but I believe it may have been picked up from the soldiers surrounding England's Buckingham Palace. New soldiers would "push" men going off duty out of their guard boxes and replace them.

Nothing on the Reagan ranch was permanently improved by the American taxpayer, and I'm sure the trailer we lived in has been removed because the Reagans didn't own it and weren't anxious to have it on their property. This attitude differs from that of President Richard Nixon, who had the U.S. government build a brick "communications house" next to the swimming pool at his home in San Clemente, California, some 135 miles south of the Reagan ranch. Mr. Nixon's "communications house" was converted to become a bath-house, and Mr. Nixon later gave the government $350,000 to pay for it.

There was also a cottage on the ranch, occupied by the caretaker, Lee Clearwater, who died of a heart attack several months after I arrived. His body was found by his wife, who had returned for the weekend after having worked as a nurse in nearby Santa Barbara. President Reagan was in Washington at the time, and was quite shocked to get the news of Clearwater's death. When he told me, I suggested that before he hired any future caretakers he let me give them a physical examination to make sure they were in good health.

There was a helicopter landing pad and hangar a few thousand yards from the Reagan's home next to a radio beacon on a mountain-top. This vector station helps airplanes flying down the coast make their turn toward Los Angeles. I believe it's on land the government rents from the Reagans. The Marine pilots, who were on duty, stayed up there, as did the White House communications team with its transmission equipment. I used to walk up there every morning and evening along what they call the Vector Road, always informing the Secret Service beforehand so they wouldn't take me for an intruder.

When the president was at his ranch, he and the First Lady would usually take a morning ride, choosing one of several dirt trails depending on whether they wanted to be seen by press photographers with their telephoto lenses at the ready. President Reagan uses a smooth English saddle, and the First Lady a Western one with a roping horn up front. Horseback riding is not her favorite pastime, but she goes along, riding a fairly docile horse, because her husband loves it and could ride forever astride his big white horse El Alamein.

Before he became governor of California, Ronald Reagan belonged to a group called the Rancheros Vistadores, who rode horses with silver saddles in the Rose Bowl Parade, and on excursions into the hills where they'd camp out at night. There was plenty of good food and a bar, so it wasn't exactly roughing it. But Mr. Reagan enjoyed it and may have rejoined the group now that he's a private citizen again.

Ray Shaddick, who was President Reagan's number one bodyguard and held the same job with President Bush, ordered me not to join the Reagans on their horseback rides around the ranch. Ray was afraid that if someone took a shot at the president, the horses might gallop off in all directions, or I might get hit and possibly killed. So I always rode a discreet distance behind the president in a Jeep loaded with a first-aid kit, stretchers, a neck brace, traction gear, and other medical equipment. I was ready for just about anything. The White House Communications Agency van carrying my nurse was also within hailing distance, and was equipped with telephones the president could use to call anywhere in the world, which might prove useful in the event of a medical emergency.

The president's HMX1 helicopter was nearby in case we needed to rush him to Cottage Hospital in Santa Barbara about fourteen minutes away by air. There was a closer hospital in the little town of Solvang, but I had checked it out and found it was too small for our purposes. It had no cardiac care unit, no intensive care unit, and no well-rounded medical staff.

It was absolutely vital that we take all these precautions to protect the president, yet in the two years I was with him, I was never called on to give him, or Mrs. Reagan, so much as a Band-Aid. The greatest emergency I had at the ranch was when a Secret Service Jeep flipped over and one of the agents sustained a bad cut on his forehead. In an accident like this you assume the person has a broken neck, so I put a neck brace on him and had him taken to the Santa Barbara hospital by ambulance.

While the Secret Service agents knew how much the president loved to ride his horse, I think they were much happier when he was driving around in his old beat-up Jeep which he dearly loved, or in the new red Ford Ranger utility vehicle the Reagans had given each other for Christmas in 1985.

President Reagan knew how sensitive I was about his health, and he wasn't above having a little fun with me. Every now and then, when he saw me coming down the hill toward the stables where he was saddling El Alamein, he'd grab his chest and pretend to sink to the ground as if he'd just been shot or was having a heart attack. But the big grin on his face told me I had no reason to worry, although I did worry and asked him please not to scare me that way again.

I told the president I thought he should wear a wide-brimmed cowboy hat when riding or doing chores in order to keep the sun off his face, since I didn't want any precancerous spots to reappear similar to the one we had removed from his nose. But he refused, saying he was not a cowboy, and wanted no part of cowboy hats, Western chaps, or saddles. I knew I was beaten on the cowboy hat, so we compromised on a peaked cap, and on sunblock whenever he rode or played golf.

President Reagan saw himself as a cavalryman, at home in an English saddle and habit, and proficient at a cavalry dismount. He'd slide off his horse, land on both feet, and snap to attention. On one occasion, however, he dismounted on a log he obviously hadn't seen, causing him to fall, and that ended that act. President Reagan thought the disappearance of the cavalry was the worst thing that ever happened because so many good Army veterinarians were lost and a lot of excellent animal care with them.

One-Way Airfare $3 Million

Somebody told me it cost $3 million to fly the president aboard Air Force One from Washington to California's U.S. Naval Air Station at Point Magu, or less often to Los Angeles International Airport, and then on to his ranch, often called the Western White House. This could be the reason he usually scheduled one or two official stops along the way to the ranch to help justify the cost of the trip, which could then be defrayed by the Republican party or the State Department.

The presidential helicopter, plus two similar choppers for members of the White House staff and press corps, were flown to California so they'd be there when the Reagans arrived. Since they can fly only a few hundred miles before they need to be refueled, they'd have to leave Washington days ahead of the president, barnstorming across the United States from one military base to another until they reached Los Angeles, which provided good training for the Marine pilots.

I loved the low-level helicopter flight from the Los Angeles airport to the Reagan ranch even though some economy-conscious aide to the president must have suggested saving money by using smaller Huey helicopters whose rotors fold up so they could be flown to California in a cargo plane. This was done, but the Hueys are so small that it's virtually impossible to move without disturbing someone, which usually means the president of the United States or the First Lady.

When I sat opposite the president we'd have to intertwine our legs to be comfortable, and I was equally ill at ease when perched on the narrow seat opposite the exit door since my knees were wedged up against it. On one flight I was seated next to a big Secret Service man, had my medical bag and a small suitcase on my lap, and was practically touching the First Lady's head. Suddenly my hay fever started acting up, my nose began to drip, and I desperately needed to sneeze, yet couldn't get a hand into my pocket to grab a handkerchief or up to my nose to stifle the sneeze. So I just prayed I could hold out until we landed, and my prayers were answered.

As we skimmed along from the Los Angeles airport to the Reagan ranch, I'd peer down at places that meant the world to me: my house in Brentwood, with its tennis court that I had played on almost every day; the Los Angeles Country Club, where I'd been a member for years; the beautiful Beach Club, where I regularly paid my dues even though I hadn't been there since moving to Washington; and then out over the Channel Islands, where I'd been in more sail boat races than I could recall.

The president enjoyed looking down at familiar landmarks every bit as much as I did, and would draw my attention to some of his favorite spots such as "Kerosene Point" near Santa Barbara, which he said used to be touted as a health spa where people would come to "take the waters." The elixir in those waters was undoubtedly petroleum, as a major oil field was discovered not far from that very point along the coast.

President Reagan's greatest thrill, however, was catching the first sight of his ranch, where he'd soon be riding his horse, doing some physical work clearing the land around his house, and generally relaxing the instant the helicopter touched the ground. I remember one trip when the fog was so thick he couldn't even see the ranch as we approached it. But then the famous "Reagan luck" took hold, the clouds parted, and we landed without incident only to have the fog roll in again the moment we were safely on the ground.

The president would spend part of the afternoon doing ranch chores like clearing brush and chopping wood, and since I had to be nearby I'd often work along with him. Every now and then we'd take a break, sit on a log, and he'd talk about caring for horses, riding horses, cattle, gold mining, early California history, the old days in Hollywood— anything but politics and affairs of state. One time he pointed to a leafy green plant and said it was called "miner's lettuce" because it was the closest they could get to the real thing during the California gold rush.

I insisted the president wear safety glasses when chopping wood, and both glasses and earplugs when using a chain saw, which made a hellish noise and was often tough to start. This caused him to cuss like an old Army cavalry trooper before giving in and asking William "Barney" Barnett, who came up to the ranch to help out whenever the president was there, to start it for him (Barney had a knack for getting the thing going). Barney was a retired California Highway Patrol officer who drove Ronald Reagan when he was governor and continued to call him "Governor" even after he became president. The Reagans thought the world of Barney, and would invite him to join them for dinner whenever he was working around the ranch.

When the president and First Lady were staying at the ranch, their meals were prepared by Anne, the cook, who drove up from Los Angeles. Anne was a terrific cook who baked great cookies (usually leaving a plate for us inside the back door of the ranch house). Anne would occasionally bring a plate of cookies, or something left over from dinner, up to our trailer as a special treat.

Life was pleasant and generally uneventful on the Reagan ranch for both the military aide and myself. We'd prepare our own breakfast and lunch in the trailer from supplies one of Eddie Serrano's people named Joe had brought us. Joe would come up again in the late afternoon and cook our dinner with food he'd buy for us in Santa Barbara (always keeping within the $30-a-day allowance each of us was given for food supplies). One Thanksgiving Day, President Reagan strolled over to our trailer and gave us a bottle of wine to go with our turkey dinner, which I couldn't enjoy since I was a strict teetotaler on the job.

Celebrating the Holidays in California

We rarely left the ranch when we were there, although one Sunday the Reagans did attend Easter church services in the nearby crossroads village of Solvang to mark the fifth anniversary of his surviving the assassination attempt on his life.

President and Mrs. Reagan would always spend Christmas in Washington, D.C., with nursing home tycoon Charles Z. Wick and his wife, Mary Jane. Wick was the president's choice to direct the U.S. Information Agency, and I knew the family personally because our daughters had gone to school together. So when I followed the Reagans through their front door I was kissed on the cheek by Mrs. Wick, which seemed to startle the First Lady. But then I was shown to one of the Wicks' bedrooms which had been turned into a holding room. I was confined there with the communications and security people who always accompanied the president. They were all younger, read books, and didn't have much to say as we waited for the Wicks and their guests to finish dinner, exchange gifts, and sing Christmas carols.

The Reagans would fly into the Palm Springs airport just before New Year's, and then motorcade to Rancho Mirage, where they'd spend several days at Sunnylands, the sprawling 350-acre estate of their friends Walter and Lenore Annenberg on the corner of Bob Hope and Frank Sinatra drives. Walter Annenberg owned the company that published *TV Guide* (which he sold in 1988 for $3 billion), and had been President Reagan's choice for ambassador to Great Britain; Mrs. Annenberg was made White House chief of protocol.

The Annenbergs' estate is surrounded by a high fence covered with white, rose, and purple oleanders, and protected by television surveillance cameras and security men. The president was able to walk around the estate in complete safety, including on its golf course, where he'd regularly play with White House colleagues Don Regan and George Shultz, and some imported golf pros, including Tom Watson and Lee Trevino.

Sunnylands' main house has a soaring atrium, Spanish tile floors covered with exquisite carpets, and walls hung with paintings from the Annenbergs' extraordinary collection of art, which includes notable works by Vincent van Gogh, Paul Gauguin, Claude Monet, Edgar Degas, Pierre-Auguste Renoir, Henri de Toulouse-Lautrec, and other great Impressionists and Postimpressionists.

In the back of the main house are four guest houses attached by breezeways. When we were there they were occupied by the Reagans and two of their closest friends: William Wilson (whom the president appointed ambassador to the Vatican) and his wife, Betty, and steel tycoon Earle Jorgensen and his wife, Marion.

A little further away are three apartments each with a sitting room, two bedrooms, two baths, a kitchen, a garage, golf carts to get back and forth to the main house, a direct telephone line to the temporary Palm Springs White House switchboard to handle all calls, and a maid to cook meals, do the laundry, and keep the place tidy. British ambassador Price and his wife stayed in one, the military aide with the "football" and I stayed in another, and the head of the Secret Service contingent guarding the president stayed in the third.

When I could arrange some free time, I would drive over to Marrakesh Country Club, where Kit and I have a desert home. Our whole family enjoyed the setting, weather, golf, tennis, and swimming. Here we found an ideal pace to live and many friends who fully enjoyed living there; truly the "jewel of the desert." With my confinement in Washington, we had leased the property for an indefinite period. However, it was always exhilarating to wander around and greet friends.

The day the president and First Lady arrived at Sunnylands, everybody would go to El Dorado Country Club for dinner hosted by the Wilsons and Jorgensens in a private room holding about sixty people located off the main dining room. The room was nicely decorated with round tables, and back in the kitchen Eddie Serrano was supervising the chefs preparing the meal.

The presidential motorcade from the Annenberg estate would drive up, and awaiting it were a roomful of guests who were eagerly anticipating his arrival, including some who had brought their children along to share this auspicious occasion. The invited guests would move on to a cocktail reception, where they would all mix, mingle, and chat rather than have the president and First Lady stand in a receiving line. Four or more Secret Service men dressed in black tie moved around the room, with Ray Shaddick always beside the president.

I'd stay with the rest of the staff in a room adjoining the cocktail party, and when the presidential party left to have dinner, we'd go into the cocktail room, where dinner had been set up for us. But the last year I was there, friends of ours, Helen and Philip Fowler, who were members of the club, invited Kit and me to join them for dinner in the main dining room, which seats about 175 people (all of whom had stepped through a metal detector to make sure they weren't carrying weapons).

As President and Mrs. Reagan and their party walked through the main dining room toward a private room, all the club members and their guests would stand up and applaud. The most memorable dinner the El Dorado Club's chefs knew how to prepare was then beautifully served, and the moment it was over, all the club members and their families started leaving for home and bed, which is traditional in the desert. I felt President Reagan was disappointed when he and his guests returned through the main dining room to see that all the club members had left, the lights had been dimmed, the tables were empty, the room was quiet, and a delightful evening was at an end even though it was only around 9:30.

Chapter Eleven

White House Family Doctor

Whenever I wasn't traveling with the president, I could be found on duty with my White House medical staff ready to look after anyone who needed help.

My first priority was President Ronald Reagan and Vice President George Bush. But as the White House family doctor, I also cared for anyone in the president's home who had a medical problem; examining, advising, and if necessary referring the individual to outside doctors. This applied to members of President Reagan's cabinet, his guests, military personnel (for whom I established a special medical clinic in the Old Executive Office Building), and tourists.

The White House, as far as I know, is the only head of state's home that's open to the public, and several weekday mornings, hundreds of people line up to get in. They stand for up to three hours in winter's bitter cold or in summer's boiling sun, when vacationing schoolchildren arrive in droves.

Some have driven all night to be first in line, while others have gone without breakfast and become weak, clammy, and prone to fainting because of low blood sugar. In summer, the White House put tents out on the Ellipse south of the White House and provided entertainment to help pass the time. It also upgraded the bathroom facilities, which had been inadequate. But quite a few people still fainted, and we never knew whether it was from simple exhaustion or something more serious such as a heart attack, stroke, or diabetic attack. So we'd rush out and treat them on the spot, with most reviving right away.

One benign little man in his seventies became hysterical while waiting and began punching his fists through the small panes in one of the antique glass windows in the White House's East Wing. A Secret Service man grabbed him, called me, and I came down and treated the cuts on his hands before they took him into custody. They knew he was no particular threat to the president because everyone who visits the White House goes through a metal detection device like those used in airports.

Answering the President's Mail

I had another White House job, which was to answer letters addressed to the president concerning matters of health. Anytime anything newsworthy happened to Ronald Reagan such as his operation for colon cancer, we'd be flooded with letters from all over the world suggesting various types of postoperative care, along with lots of letters saying how well he looked. Most of these letters were fairly straightforward, such as those from Mr. Reagan's friends telling him about their own cancer, and what they were doing to treat it.

Occasionally, however, some pretty eccentric letters would arrive on my desk. One suggested that the president sleep in a hospital intensive care ward every night so that if he had a heart attack he could get instant medical attention. Another warned that someone might try to slip a bomb into the batteries powering his two hearing aids. Still another recommended that President Reagan and members of his senior staff be given CAT scans to make sure their brains were "working right." While CAT scans of the brain cannot reveal how the brain is working, or if it's making the proper decisions, it can disclose anatomical abnormalities. A CAT scan, for example, might have spotted the brain tumor growing inside Central Intelligence Agency Director William Casey's head early on and could have conceivably saved his life.

Ronald Reagan received quite a few letters asking him to see, write, or talk to people, mainly children, suffering from severe burns, leukemia, cancer, and other terminal conditions before they died. Each of these "last wish" letters were sent to me to check before telling the president it was all right to chat with these individuals on the telephone, send them a letter and an autographed picture, or invite them to visit him in the White House to help lift their spirits.

My mission was to find out if these letters were legitimate. I did this by talking to each person's doctor, family, and others, thus saving the president the embarrassment of contacting someone who didn't know what he was talking about, and might not even want to hear from him. I'd also follow up to find out what had become of these children, since the president would usually ask me, "Whatever happened to that little boy I saw a few weeks ago?" and I'd too often have to say, "Oh, I'm afraid he died, Mr. President."

One cross I had to bear was that people were constantly asking me to get personal messages to President Reagan. I remember once when Don Regan made a nasty crack about nuns who work in Catholic hospitals, saying something like, "They're lovely people, but they don't know what they're doing because their heads aren't screwed on right." There happened to be a meeting of Catholic hospital representatives going on in Washington at the time, and two nuns I knew from Saint John's Hospital in Los Angeles where I had practiced called me to ask if I'd please tell the president they didn't like what his chief of staff had said about nuns. Of course, I didn't discuss this with the president.

I had quite a few friends who wanted to drop by when I was in Washington, many of them doctors in town for medical meetings. I'd ask if they'd ever been to the White House, and if not I'd invite them over after 5:30 P.M. when the president usually finished work in the Oval Office and went upstairs to the White House residence.

My wife, Kit, would pick the doctors up at their meeting or hotel, and drive them to the White House, where they'd be admitted through the Southwest Gate. I'd meet them there, and give them a little talk as we walked to a spot on the lawn outside the West Wing entrance where you could see the White House, Lafayette Square, the New Executive Office Building, and the Old Executive Office Building. Vice President Bush worked in the Old Executive Office Building in what used to be the secretary of the Navy's office. President Nixon also used this office when secretly taping conversations with his staff and visitors, which eventually led to the Watergate crisis and his resignation.

I'd tell the visiting doctors how the main White House was the first to be built, followed by the West Wing and the Executive Office Building, and how these three buildings contained the president's entire staff, the State Department, and most of the military services when forty-two-year-old Theodore Roosevelt moved into the White House in 1901 following the assassination of President William McKinley.

Today, the Pentagon contains more space than these three buildings combined, and even it can't hold all the military brass which has spilled over into ancillary buildings all over Washington and beyond. The State Department has its own building plus spillover space. And there must be close to 2,000 people working in White House administration in the West Wing and Executive Office Building, which together also hold a bank, credit union, post office, cafeteria, gym, and other staff conveniences.

Now and then I'd take a guest to lunch in the White House Mess reserved for senior staff including members of the president's cabinet. The mess is an intimate, oak-paneled, low-ceilinged, clubby little place run by the Navy, with paintings of famous naval ships and battles on the walls and a good menu. It costs $100 to join, and you're billed for whatever you and your guests eat and drink unless you're there on official business, as I often was when I entertained doctors to heads of state visiting President Reagan. Foreigners and journalists are barred from this dining room so the secretary of defense and others can talk about sensitive matters without fear of being overheard. I'd also lunch in the less formal junior staff mess, which had a big round "no host" table for people eating alone, and I'd routinely bump into friends such as President Reagan's last spokesman, Marlin Fitzwater, or speechwriter Peggy Noonan.

Billows of Smoke

The senior and junior White House Mess dining rooms were usually filled with cigarette and pipe smoke, and as the White House physician I was concerned about people's health, particularly the stewards who served everyone while walking around all day in this sickly haze.

The White House Press Room was also cloudy with smoke, which upset ABC White House correspondent Sam Donaldson, a reformed smoker who tried to enlist my help in getting it stopped. He wanted nicotine-addicted reporters to be exiled to another room where they could puff their hearts out while watching via television what was going on in the press room. Sam finally put a "No Smoking" sign in the press room (which was built over the old White House swimming pool), but immediately got a lot of flack from smokers who refused to stop. But then several senior members of the White House press corps developed lung cancer, had operations, came back to work, but didn't do too well. After that, a lot of smokers stepped outside the press room before lighting up.

Smoking was also a subject of debate aboard White House airplanes. Vice President Bush and the First Lady prohibited it on their planes, but the president tolerated it aboard Air Force One even though he doesn't smoke himself. He used to smoke a pipe when he was in the movies because it was the thing to do. But he gave up the habit in part because his brother, Neil, had developed cancer of the larynx from smoking.

Although smoking was allowed on Air Force One, about the only people I ever saw light up were the late Ed Hickey, who was director of the White House Military Office, and Admiral John Poindexter, the president's national security adviser who furiously puffed on a pipe, sending huge clouds of smoke throughout the cabin, which just devastated the place, although nobody ever asked him to stop.

I went to the president and asked him if he wanted me to put out an edict forbidding smoking on Air Force One, in the White House Mess, and in the White House press room. "Well," he said in his usually amiable way, "some people like to smoke, and I guess it's OK." I said, "But, Mr. President, the White House is your home and Air Force One is your plane. How do you want me to handle it?" He just said, "Do what you can, but don't worry too much about it." After I left Dr. Hutton made sure Air Force I was "smoke-free."

It was not that the president was indifferent to the hazards of smoking, but rather that he didn't want to inconvenience anyone and was aware of their rights. I found this to be one of his more admirable traits, but apparently not a positive quality when it comes to management style.

Mrs. Reagan used to say, "Ronnie is a soft sell" and felt that it was one of her responsibilities to put her foot down whenever he agreed to commitments which would overwhelm his already full schedule. I've often wondered if this might have been the origin of her antidrug slogan "Just Say No!"

Meeting the Doctors to Other Heads of State

I always tried to meet with the personal physicians to other world figures whenever they visited the president in the White House, or during our trips overseas. When a foreign dignitary was scheduled to visit President Reagan, I'd get in touch with Bunny Murdock, assistant chief of protocol for the State Department, and ask if there was going to be a doctor along. If there was, State would arrange for us to meet when the head of state the doctor was with showed up outside the president's office. Sometimes I'd invite the doctor for lunch in the White House Mess—with the State Department picking up the check—and then take the doctor down to my office for a chat. We might talk about the use of new drugs like lidocaine, which is injected intravenously to prevent fibrillation of a heart that is beating erratically and cannot pump blood efficiently to the brain and body. Or I might show a doctor some new medical gadget such as the automatic heart defibrillator I carried with me everywhere I went. This device can shock a wildly quivering heart back into a normal rhythm (otherwise the heart is not an effective pump, it's not perfusing blood to the brain, and the person may become brain dead in approximately seven minutes).

The doctors from Japan and China were particularly intrigued by this, while doctors from countries such as Tunisia, South Korea, and Mozambique were fascinated by just about any new development in American medicine because so many of them had been trained here and spoke excellent English. Prince Charles and Lady Diana brought their physician with them, and when I found out he was a urologist like myself I asked him to speak to my staff to show them that I wasn't the only urologist looking after VVIPs.

While I never did meet the physician to King Fahd of Saudi Arabia when he visited President Reagan in early February 1985, I did send one of my junior doctors over to inspect the medical setup aboard his two royal 747s when they were parked at Andrews Air Force Base next to Air Force One, which was a mere 707 at that time, and a sixteen-year-old one at that.

Air Force One has since been upgraded to a luxuriously appointed 747, and during the initial planning stages I requested space for a medical unit. I wanted enough space to store essential equipment such as a large steel tank of oxygen, movable hangers for intravenous solutions, and good overhead lighting for examining and treating passengers who became ill, plus room for a nurse and possibly a second physician should an emergency develop requiring a medical team. This is a distinct possibility since many passengers on Air Force One including the president, members of his cabinet, congressional representatives, and others are often in their sixties, seventies, and eighties when serious medical emergencies can arise without warning. On the old 707 we had no choice but to examine those who became ill in their seat or in the aisle with everyone looking on. I had hoped this could be avoided by building a medical unit into the far larger 747. But instead the plane has a multipurpose room which normally seats three people and can be quickly turned into a medical facility.

Heads of state constantly come here for medical tests and treatment, and as a courtesy they'll be admitted to our best private hospitals, or the Walter Reed Army Medical Center, where they'll pay for their own care. Walter Reed has long been the favorite of U.S. presidents (Eisenhower was frequently treated there and eventually died there from chronic coronary disease at age seventy-eight).

Allowing foreign leaders into this country for medical care, however, can have explosive consequences, as President Jimmy Carter discovered when he allowed the deposed and dying Shah of Iran to enter the United States for medical tests. The information fed to President Carter was that he could be diagnosed and treated only here, although he could have been cared for just as well in Mexico. As a result of this decision, the U.S. Embassy in Tehran was overrun and fifty-two Americans were taken hostage. They were held captive inside the embassy for 444 days, and released as Ronald Reagan was being sworn in as the fortieth president of the United States on January 20, 1981.

One of the most fascinating of my opposite numbers was Dr. M. Attia, professor of cardiology at Ain Shams University in Cairo, who was physician to Egypt's President Hosni Mubarak. Dr. Attia also served President Anwar as-Sadat and usually sat right behind him at ceremonial events in the infamous "kill zone." But on the afternoon of October 6, 1981, Sadat had invited a lot of dignitaries to join him in reviewing a military parade in Cairo, and as a result his doctor was assigned a seat seven rows higher up in the stands. This saved his life since Sadat and those around him were assassinated that day by Egyptian soldiers who broke out of the military procession, stormed the reviewing stand, and opened fire with automatic weapons and hand grenades. Dr. Attia told me he rushed Egypt's president to the nearest hospital even though they knew he was mortally wounded, and continued to operate on him, because he was head of state, even though he knew it was futile. President Reagan was unable to attend President Sadat's funeral, but he requested that former presidents Carter, Ford, and Nixon attend instead; the first time the four former presidents had traveled together.

The heroic effort to save Sadat was similar to the equally hopeless attempt to save the life of President John F. Kennedy following his assassination in Dallas. It was all over before he got to Parkland Hospital; there was no life-or-death decision to make. It was the same with efforts to revive Indian Prime Minister Indira Gandhi, whom I had met five days before she was riddled with bullets by members of her personal security guard as she walked from her home to her office in New Delhi.

When to stop trying to extend the life of a head of state is a tough call for any physician, but it's the physician's call and the physician must make it. If President Reagan had been mortally wounded following the Hinkley shooting it would have probably been up to the head surgeon who operated on him to say it's hopeless, and after one or more other doctors had concurred, the machines would have been turned off and his death announced.

Dr. Daniel Ruge, President Reagan's physician at that time, was already in his car in the motorcade, didn't know the president had been shot, and had little to do with saving his life. That responsibility fell to Jerry Parr, the Secret Service agent accompanying the president as he left the Washington Hilton Hotel. The moment Parr heard the shooting, which brought down two Washington, D.C., policemen, Secret Service agent Tim McCarthy, and presidential Press Secretary James Brady, he shoved Mr. Reagan into the back of his limousine. He then forced the president down on the floor in front of the rear seat, and jumped on top of him, bruising Mr. Reagan's ribs as his chest hit the hump covering the car's drive shaft.

Protocol in an emegency like this calls for the president to be rushed back to the sanctuary of the White House, with its communications network, which could be used to alert the nation if the shooting signaled the beginning of a conspiracy to overthrow the government, or even war. But as the limousine wheeled toward the White House, with the injured president now sitting up in the back seat, Secret Service agent Parr saw that Mr. Reagan was coughing up some pink frothy liquid, so he broke protocol and ordered the driver to turn around and head for the George Washington Hospital emergency room.

Dr. Ruge had no idea what was happening, and was appalled when he saw the president's car going in the opposite direction from his own. But Jerry Parr did the right thing. It was a great call, and it undoubtedly saved President Reagan's life because by the time they got him out of the car and into the White House, I think he might have bled out and died. One of the amazing aspects of this whole episode was that nobody knew the president had been shot, including the president. He told me repeatedly, "I don't remember being shot."

It's interesting to note, by the way, that the man who almost killed President Reagan is now saying that it wouldn't have happened if there had been a law requiring a waiting period before he could buy a gun.

An Associated Press story dated August 7, 1989, quoted John W. Hinkley, Jr., as saying, "I was responding to a paradoxical rage induced by the constant use of Valium," and if a waiting period had been required, "I believe I would not have gone forward with the effort to shoot the president."

Emergency Medical Drills

I was amazed to find out that the Secret Service had not been drilled with the White House medical unit on how best to handle medical emergencies. Medicine, like the military, is based on constant practice. Everything has to go according to plan, and if it doesn't, lives can be lost. You can't believe the panic that goes on when a president is shot. People become hysterical and run around in circles. It's dreadful. I decided to try and do something about it when I got to the White House by constantly drilling my doctors and nurses with the Secret Service agents so that handling any type of medical emergency would become second nature. We wouldn't even have to think about what to do. I fabricated scenarios where members of the presidential party broke their necks and their legs, had heart attacks, and were hit with machine gun fire or exploding bombs. And to add to the chaos I had people countermanding our orders and trying to divert us in every way they could think of because as doctors we're supposed to keep our minds on the job, always working in a logical sequence to save the patient's life.

I had a male Secret Service agent play the part of President Reagan, and a female agent stand in for the First Lady. We pretended the president had been shot and, as often happens in real life, the First Lady would bang on my back screaming, "Is he going to be all right?" [bang]. "Is he going to die?" [bang]. "You've got to save him, doctor" [bang]. I ran these emergency scenarios in the motorcade, in the White House, at Camp David, aboard Air Force One (where we practiced getting the president out of the plane and into an ambulance), everywhere I could think of when the president wasn't there.

I had to get special permission to run these drills at the Reagan ranch in California because that's his private property. I told the president we had to know how to get an ambulance up there, how to get a helicopter down in case of evacuation, and so on. He said, "OK, just don't leave any dead bodies around."

One of the unexpected benefits of these drills was that they brought my medical unit and the Secret Service closer together than they'd been before. The Secret Service thought this was a useful exercise for them, and when it was over, they gave me a certificate of appreciation, which hangs on the wall of my study along with those the president gave me whenever we returned from a trip abroad.

The Limits of Medicine

I kept thinking how fortunate President Reagan was since although seriously wounded by John W. Hinkley, Jr., he suffered no serious aftereffects as former Alabama Governor George Wallace has from the moment he was shot by Arthur Bremer on May 16, 1972, while campaigning for the Democratic presidential nomination in Laurel, Maryland.

This attempt on Governor Wallace's life left him a paraplegic confined to a wheelchair. He has also been in constant, often incapacitating pain for twenty years, which a series of operations has failed to end. I remember reading that Governor Wallace was scheduled to enter the hospital for yet another operation around the time President Reagan returned to the White House on July 20, 1985, following his surgery for colon cancer. That was thirteen years after Governor Wallace had been shot, and it wasn't to be his last operation by any means.

Nations go to extraordinary lengths to keep their leaders alive even though there are limits to medicine like everything else. This was vividly demonstrated by the doctors looking after Japan's dying Emporer Hirohito, whom they kept technically alive by continuously transfusing him with fresh blood.

The limits of medicine are sometimes compromised when desperate doctors try to bring a president back from a serious illness too fast. This happened late in the evening of March, 14, 1985, just a few weeks after I started work in the White House, when Brazil's President-elect Tancredo Neves was rushed to a hospital in Brasília just before his inauguration with what looked like a benign intestinal tumor with some evidence of septicemia.

Brazilians were full of hope for the Neves regime, which represented a return to democracy after twenty-one years of military rule. Mr. Neves's doctors were eager to get him on his feet for the inauguration. But the man was seventy-five years old, about the same age as President Reagan, and when his condition failed to improve after a second operation, he was flown to another hospital in São Paulo, where press reports say he underwent seven more operations. His bacterial infection began affecting his lungs and kidneys, forcing his doctors to keep him under heavy sedation. But his heart continued to weaken, and on April 21, 1985, he died because they tried to cut corners and it caught up with them.

The trouble was that Tancredo Neves was a VVIP and his doctors moved too fast. They should have let his condition quiet down, gone back weeks or months later when he was finally ready, and done the surgery in a more conservative manner.

Celebrating the UN's Fortieth Anniversary

I doubt if there have been many times in history when as many presidents, prime ministers, kings, and queens converged upon one place as those who came to New York City toward the end of 1985 to celebrate the fortieth anniversary of the United Nations. Hundreds of security agents and limousines—not to mention dozens of doctors like me accompanying the world's leaders—threatened to turn the East Side of Manhattan into permanent "limo-lock" making it a hair-raising experience for chauffeurs trying to get their magnificos to the UN in time to give their speeches.

I was with President Reagan as he took off from Washington at 9:20 A.M. on October 23 aboard Air Force One, flew to New York, helicoptered to the foot of Wall Street, and motorcaded up the normally busy East River Drive, which had been cleared of traffic. We arrived at the U.S. Mission across from UN headquarters at noon, and within minutes President Reagan was sitting down with several other national leaders he had invited to join him for lunch followed by an afternoon of whirlwind diplomacy.

A UN reception for heads of state was scheduled for later in the afternoon, and to get to it President Reagan had to climb into his motorcade for the ten-second ride across New York's First Avenue to the UN. Next stop was the presidential suite at the Waldorf Astoria and one-on-one meetings with British Prime Minister Margaret Thatcher, Pakistani President Muhammad Zia-ul-Haq, and Indian Prime Minister Rajiv Gandhi. President Reagan then changed clothes and hosted a reception for heads of state in which he talked about the speech he planned to give at the UN the next morning.

The most fascinating guest at the reception was the then revolutionary leader of Nicaragua Daniel Ortega, whom Ronald Reagan had once described as "the little dictator who went to Moscow in his green fatigues to receive a bear hug." Nicaragua is one of the poorest countries in Latin America, yet Ortega moved around Manhattan in a seventeen-car motorcade, which came to a halt at one point so he could jump out and buy $3,500 worth of designer sunglasses.

The president and First Lady had a suite in the Waldorf Astoria Tower, and my room was next door. This time Kit was with me, but she had to fly to New York on her own and stay at another hotel nearby. Once the Reagans had retired and everything was secure, I'd go downstairs and we'd have dinner together in the Waldorf's main dining room. Then Kit would go back to her hotel, and I'd go back upstairs to my room during the two nights we were there.

New York City police had closed off First Avenue on the morning President Reagan was to address the UN, and as 10 A.M. approached he again climbed into his motorcade for the trip across the street. UN Secretary General Javier Pérez de Cuellar introduced the president, who spoke about the need to reduce tensions wherever they existed in the world, but particularly between the U.S. and the U.S.S.R. This reflected a fundamental change in his attitude toward the Soviet Union. In 1983 he had called it an "evil empire." But now he wanted to improve relations with the Soviets, and was determined that he and Premier Mikhail Gorbachev should hold a get-acquainted meeting without delay.

The New York trip had gone off without a hitch until Eddie Serrano, the president's majordomo, got trapped in the Waldorf Astoria Tower just as we were leaving town. The Waldorf had a private elevator for the exclusive use of the president, which the Secret Service sealed off so strangers couldn't go poking around the president's suite after he left. Unfortunately, Eddie, who was responsible for getting the Reagans' bags down to the motorcade, was trapped up there. By this time we were speeding down to the Battery heliport for the flight back to Washington. When word of Eddie's predicament reached us, we slowed the president's motorcade to a snail's pace, meandered around the Wall Street area, and sat waiting in the helicopter until Eddie and the luggage finally arrived in another car. Air Force One was finally airborne at 12:30 P.M., and flew directly to Andrews Air Force Base in Washington, where we transferred to a helicopter for the trip to Camp David, arriving there at 2 P.M. In just ninety minutes we had gone from the frantic police-escorted motorcades and nonstop high-level meetings in New York to the calm, secure, and relaxed atmosphere of Camp David. I found it remarkable.

Meeting Mikhail Gorbachev

President Reagan waited less than a month before making good on his determination to meet with Soviet Premier Mikhail Gorbachev by arranging for their one-on-one summit meeting to take place in Geneva, Switzerland, November 19–21, 1985.

Gorbachev at fifty-four was the youngest man to rule the Soviet Union since Stalin, and a physical and intellectual powerhouse compared to his three aged, ill, and ineffectual predecessors: Konstantin Chernenko, Yuri Andropov, and Leonid Brezhnev. Gorbachev was also twenty years younger than Ronald Reagan, and although he had been in office only eight months, he was already being heralded as the most dynamic Soviet leader in a generation.

Ronald Reagan is pretty dynamic himself, and as we headed for Geneva to meet Gorbachev, we knew the president held some very strong cards. While the United States and the Soviet Union were about equal militarily at that time, we were far stronger economically and nobody knew this better than Gorbachev, who used to head Soviet agriculture and was well aware that his country couldn't even feed itself.

We knew we had an edge, and everything was done to increase it. The president and First Lady were housed in Prince Karim Aga Khan's luxurious villa called the Maison de Saussure, overlooking Lake Geneva. The president was surrounded by aides who were both younger and more fashionably dressed than the Soviets.

It was planned to have the talks between the two leaders take place at the Villa Fleur d'Eau, another big lakeside mansion that we rented and then spruced up. Although it was a cold gray day, millions of television viewers worldwide saw a coatless and hatless President Reagan stride down the stairs of the villa at 10 A.M. to greet Gorbachev as he emerged from his limousine bundled up in overcoat, scarf, and fedora. Then, without missing a beat, the president put his hand on Gorbachev's elbow, and helped the younger man up the stairs and into the meeting.

President Reagan had already strolled around the grounds of the Villa Fleur d'Eau looking for a good place for him and Gorbachev to hold their talk. He finally found it in a delightful pool house with warm fireplace just a short stroll from the main house. This proved to be an ideal setting for what turned out to be the longest private session in fourteen years of U.S.-Soviet summits. Reagan and Gorbachev pulled up two chairs before a crackling fire, and talked for fifty-four minutes with only interpreters present. While all the discussions in Geneva were cordial, they ended in disagreement over the president's insistence on developing the space-based Star Wars weapons system, which Gorbachev saw as a threat to Soviet security.

The staffs of the two leaders also compared notes in Geneva including, believe it or not, the men who carried their nation's "footballs," and chatted about such things as how many communications channels each had available in the event of a nuclear emergency. While in Geneva I had my first chance to meet, and communicate through translators when chatting, with Gorbachev's young, always smiling personal physician, going from English, to French, to Russian, and back again.

At one point, senior Soviet staff people in the holding room invited us to join them for caviar and ice-cold vodka. We couldn't enjoy the caviar, however, because our hosts had forgotten to bring any spoons, so I improvised by passing around wooden tongue depressers from my medical bag. I never did get to try the vodka because I never drank on duty, and rarely off duty.

The Secret Service did its usual thorough job of protecting the president in Geneva as I learned firsthand every night when sharpshooters came to my room located on the third floor of Maison de Saussure right above the Reagans. They'd stand on my bed and peer out my window using infrared binoculars which could pick up the body heat of intruders approaching the maison on land, or from boats on Lake Geneva.

On our second evening in Geneva I had an opportunity to meet Premier Gorbachev and his wife, Raisa, at a reception for the U.S. and Soviet delegations held by the president of Switzerland in his official residence, La Gondole. Members of President Reagan's staff lined up alphabetically—Smith, Speakes, etc.—to shake hands with Mr. Gorbachev, and when my turn came I bowed slightly from the waist, looked him in the eye, said, "I'm the president's personal physician" (which was translated into Russian by his interpreter), and got a very firm handshake. The usual photographs were taken, and this high point of the trip for me was suddenly over.

I felt this first meeting between President Reagan and Premier Gorbachev was a success. The world's two most powerful leaders seemed to get along well. They agreed that something had to be done to reduce the threat of nuclear war (and that they were the ones to do it). And they agreed to meet again to continue their search for peace.

Chapter Twelve

The Long Road Home

Within weeks after returning from Geneva, Ronald Reagan experienced two of the saddest days of his eight years in the White House.

On December 12, 1985, a planeload of 258 Americans—all but eight members of the 101st Airborne Division returning home for Christmas from their peacekeeping duties in the Sinai Peninsula separating Egypt and Israel—were killed when their plane crashed on takeoff from Newfoundland, Canada.

Then, just seven weeks later, the Challenger space shuttle exploded on takeoff from Cape Canaveral, Florida, killing all seven astronauts aboard including Christa McAuliffe, a high school teacher from Concord, New Hampshire, who was to have been the first ordinary citizen in space.

The president and First Lady attended separate memorial services with the loved ones of those lost in both tragedies. They moved among them, comforted them with words, shook their hands, and embraced them. It was incredibly moving, and I will never forget it.

It wasn't long after these unhappy events that the president was off traveling again to the Tokyo economic summit, the Statue of Liberty's 100th birthday celebration in New York harbor, and then on to Iceland for a second meeting with Soviet Premier Mikhail Gorbachev.

Meeting Emperor Hirohito at the Summit

On April 26, 1986, President Reagan left on a twelve-day trip to attend the Association of South East Asia Nations (ASEAN) conference on the tropical island of Bali, Indonesia, and the Tokyo economic summit in Japan. We were always given background briefing books on these trips, and the book for this one was nearly a foot thick with sections on general information, Indonesia/ASEAN information, general summit information, economic summit information, economic summit overview, trade, finance, debt and monetary issues, bilateral relations, and other issues.

Our first stop after leaving Washington was the Century Plaza Hotel in Los Angeles. Air Force One would fly into the nearby Los Angeles International Airport, where we'd transfer to the president's helicopter, which used to land in a playing field next to the Beverly Hills High School. The big chopper's rotors were so powerful, however, that on one occasion they blew some of the ceramic tiles off the school's roof, and Uncle Sam got the bill to have them replaced. After that we landed on a vacant lot behind the hotel.

President Reagan liked to spend a day or two at the Century Plaza Hotel when traveling to the Far East so he could begin adjusting his biological clock. I took advantage of one of these stopovers to get his hearing checked by Drs. John and Howard House, who founded the famed House Hearing Institute in midtown Los Angeles. Ronald Reagan's hearing had been damaged when a handgun was fired too close to his right ear during his early days as a Hollywood movie actor. The president wore a hearing aid in his right ear when I arrived at the White House (and three months later he started using one in his left ear to achieve balance). But he complained to me that he was having trouble hearing people at his table during White House banquets because of the buzz in his hearing aid created by crowds of people talking and dishes clattering. This disturbed him tremendously, and he'd try to get rid of it by turning his hearing aid down, which made it even more difficult to catch conversations going on around him. The Houses finally solved the problem by getting him an advanced-design hearing aid made by Siemens, which filtered out all the lower-decibel background noise.

When I first began looking after President Reagan, we used a motorcade to take him from the Century Plaza Hotel to the House Hearing Institute, some fifteen minutes away (with a Los Angeles Police Department motorcycle escort clearing the way as we went). We all felt guilty about this because the president's motorcade had already completely shut down the big freeway leading from the airport to the hotel. It was eerie. There were no other cars anywhere around us as we rolled merrily along one of the most heavily traveled highways in the world.

This had local motorists steaming, and so as not to make matters worse, we decided to have the House brothers visit the president at the Century Plaza. The only people upset by this decision were members of the president's LAPD motorcycle escort, who loved to clear the way when he traveled. They'd all line up beside his motorcade, the president would give them a "Hi" as he got into his limousine, an aide would give each of them a photograph of the president, and they'd roar off down the highway happy as clams.

"Don't ever do this to me again!"

We resumed our trip to Bali by spending two days in Hawaii so we could make a second adjustment of the president's biological clock. When we were motorcading into Honolulu, the president's limousine suddenly took off for the hospital. I thought he must be having a heart attack, and the press following right behind us obviously thought the same because when we arrived in front of the hospital's main entrance the reporters, led by Helen Thomas of United Press International, rushed up to Mr. Reagan's car yelling, "Who's sick?" "What's going on?" "Has the president been shot?" The answer was that Mr. Reagan was simply granting what may have been the last wish of a little Filipino boy who had come to Honolulu with his grandmother to receive chemotherapy for leukemia, and said he'd like to talk with the president of the United States. I was irritated that neither Don Regan or Bill Henkle had told me what was going on and I told them, "Don't ever do this to me again!"

When we finally arrived in Honolulu, the president and First Lady stayed in one house on Maunolua bay in Oahu, and the military aide and I stayed in one next door (with the rest of the residential party some distance away at the Kanala Hilton Hotel). My house had a tennis court, so the first thing I did was get up games of doubles with other staff people with little to do except stand by in case they were needed. Among the eager players were the president's executive assistant Bill Henkle, the president's secretary Kathy Osborne, the head of White House staff secretary, David Chew, and White House photographer Bill Fitzpatrick. There were about a dozen tennis players in our group, including Dale Petrosky, and we managed to play all over the world from Florida to Bali.

The president and First Lady enjoyed strolling along the beach in front of their house, and the United States Coast Guard obviously felt it should protect them against someone rushing at them from the ocean. So they stationed one Coast Guardsman in a rubber boat, and had another sailor pull it along through the surf with a rope. The Coast Guard had stationed a second boat offshore beyond the reef, but the sea was so rough, and its crew was getting so queasy, that the boat left its station, marking the end of waterborne security for that day.

There was a couple sleeping face down on the beach, and as the Reagans walked by, one of them looked up and said, "Oh, there's the president," and went back to sleep again. This moment was captured on film by a whole array of cameramen stationed at the end of the beach. They stayed out there virtually night and day praying for a photo opportunity like that, or another one they got when the president picked up a coconut and tossed it like a football. Both incidents were worth no more than a few seconds on the nightly news.

The third adjustment of President Reagan's biological clock took place on the Pacific Island of Guam, where we had an eight-hour stopover before flying off to Bali. When we arrived there, he was completely in sync with local time and ready to get down to work.

Planning for Medical Emergencies

My major responsibility on the Bali stop of this trip, as on all others, was to plot out where we could take the president if he needed definitive medical care. We found that the nearest first-class facilities were six hours away from Bali in Manila or Singapore, eight hours away at a U.S. Navy hospital in Guam, or nine hours away in Tokyo. I decided the only option was to have another helicopter landing ship cruising six miles offshore from Bali, which the president could reach in ten to fourteen minutes.

The ship's medical staff had to be strengthened since it was limited to a surgeon, an assistant surgeon, and several nurses. So I had a top military neurosurgeon, chest surgeon, and others flown into the U.S. military base at Subic Bay in the Philippines where the ship was based.

I asked Dr. Kenneth Lee from my White House staff to come out to Subic Bay to check the ship's laboratory and its X-ray and related equipment, and to organize the old and new members of its augmented medical staff into a first-rate team as the ship was steaming toward Bali. I wanted the team in place and drilled so it would be ready to handle any emergency from the moment the president and his party arrived. Fortunately, no such emergency occurred, and the imported doctors were flown home shortly after Air Force One was airborne for Tokyo.

The First Lady was with us on this trip, but was going to leave and fly to Bangkok, Thailand, to talk about drugs with Queen Sirikit and then rejoin us in Tokyo at the end of the summit. So, I asked myself, do I advise the First Lady to go on her own to a place like Thailand, which has a small Seventh-Day Adventist Hospital, a U.S. State Department doctor whose competence I couldn't vouch for, and a group of Thai doctors I wasn't sure I wanted to turn loose on Mrs. Reagan if she became ill or was injured. I decided I simply couldn't take the chance. So I told Dr. Hutton to fly out to be with her, which meant I had only Dr. Savage back in Washington to look after Vice President Bush, whom I knew would stay close to home while the president was overseas.

An Eerie Arrival in Tokyo

Our arrival in Japan for the Tokyo economic summit was uneventful. But as the president's motorcade approached normally bustling Tokyo itself, we found the highways were deserted, and the area around the Hotel Okura where we were staying almost completely devoid of cars and pedestrians. This great city of nine million people had been virtually shut down, and its normal complement of police reinforced by thousands of additional civilian and military security people flown in from all over the country. Despite this overwhelming show of force, a group of terrorists managed to rent an apartment overlooking the main highway into town from which they fired four rockets at arriving dignitaries. Fortunately, the rockets landed harmlessly in the street.

At the urging of the United States, the leaders of the six other major industrial democracies agreed upon a summit statement condemning international terrorism as a scourge that "must be fought relentlessly and without compromise," although it stopped short of endorsing military actions or economic sanctions.

This was the first time the Japanese had played host to an economic summit of the leaders of Britain, Canada, France, Italy, West Germany, and the United States, and Prime Minister Yasuhiro Nakasone was determined to do it up right, including an invitation to dine with the emperor.

Dinner was held at the Imperial Palace set among two hundred forty-seven acres of woods, gardens, pavilions, and pools in what has to be the world's most expensive piece of real estate, located in the middle of downtown Tokyo. We arrived at the palace at 7:15 P.M., and were greeted in a quiet, intensely formal way by Emperor Hirohito's eldest son and heir, Crown Prince Akihito. The leaders met the emperor in one of the palace's audience rooms; the traditional photo opportunity was held, followed by an introduction to the imperial family.

There was a hushed, mystical air inside the palace as our Japanese hosts glided about in white tie and tails as if on a cloud. President Reagan and the other heads of state were then taken upstairs to dinner and entertainment, while we staff people were herded downstairs for a meal in the basement.

Flying Toward a Nuclear Cloud

When the president was getting ready to fly home from the Tokyo economic summit, I got word that a nuclear cloud from the April 26, 1986, explosion at the Soviet Union's Chernobyl atomic energy plant in the Ukraine was drifting toward Alaska where we planned to stop on our way back to Washington. I drew this to the attention of Chief of Staff Don Regan, in case he wanted to have a plane equipped with monitoring devices fly on ahead of us to make sure it was safe, or divert Air Force One to another destination. I don't know what Don did, but he obviously had been told that everything was safe because we flew right through to Alaska as originally planned.

Celebrating Miss Liberty's 100th Birthday

July 4, 1986, was one of the more pleasant days of Ronald Reagan's presidency as he and the First Lady flew to New York to celebrate the 100th birthday of a completely refurbished Statue of Liberty, given to us by the French in 1886. In the morning, the president boarded the battleship USS *Iowa* to survey the twenty U.S. and twenty-one foreign warships in the harbor along with hundreds of other vessels from tall sailing ships to rowboats. Mr. Reagan met with French President François Mitterand over lunch, and that night joined millions of others enjoying a spectacular twenty-eight-minute fireworks display.

Sad News from Home

Several weeks after this memorable day in New York City, I learned my younger brother, Russell, was dying of inoperable cancer and decided it was time for me to return home to California.

I was given the news of my brother's terminal illness by Dr. Donald Skinner, a urologist I had worked with at the University of California (Los Angeles) Medical Center. Dr. Skinner was part of a team that had performed four operations on my brother and was preparing to do a fifth when they found his cancer was so extensive it made no sense to proceed.

My brother had been waging his private war on cancer for fifteen years. He was a surgeon like me, and I've always felt it must be devastating for someone with his knowledge of medicine to have this terrible disease. He knew the odds and the complications and could undoubtedly visualize the tumor cells growing and spreading from one organ of his body to the next. But Russell was fighting this battle, and although he was a good sport about it he continued to go downhill.

I wanted to be near both Russell, who lived in Los Angeles, and my mother, who was ninety-eight and lived about an hour away in Palos Verdes. While my mother enjoyed good mental health, she required constant attention, which Russell could no longer provide because he was now too weary to endure the long drive to be with her.

My decision to return home was made easier by the fact that President Reagan was in good health. We had just finished examining him a year after his surgery and found him to be free of cancer and in generally good physical condition. So I went to Chief of Staff Don Regan and asked him how I should go about resigning. "You write the president a letter," he said, "and we will present it to him."

The Iceland Summit

On August 30, 1986, before I had a chance get my letter of resignation into the president's hands, the Soviets seized *U.S. News & World Report*'s Moscow Bureau Chief Nicholas Daniloff on trumped-up charges. It wasn't until September 12 that Daniloff was freed in exchange for Soviet physicist Gennadi Zakharov, allowing President Reagan's important second summit meeting with Mikhail Gorbachev to take place in Reykjavík, Iceland, on October 11 and 12.

Some progress on the key question of arms reduction had been made a year earlier in Geneva, and hopes were high that a major step toward world peace could be taken in Reykjavík. But this summit, much more than the one in Geneva, collapsed in acrimony because of President Reagan's determination to go forward with his Strategic Defense Initiative, which he saw as a purely defensive shield, whereas Gorbachev saw it as giving the U.S. military superiority over the U.S.S.R.

I sent Dr. Savage and a male nurse on ahead of me to examine the medical situation in Iceland because on this trip we had the president, the secretary of state, the secretary of the treasury, and a whole high-powered entourage. The Icelanders have socialized medicine, and Dr. Savage found that they have a very good community hospital in Reykjavík, along with a medical school that graduates thirty-five doctors a year with many going on to Scandinavia for their specialty training. Iceland, however, has only a few doctors who are capable of handling medical emergencies, and as a result most people who need big operations go to Scandinavia or Britain. So I decided to bring in my own medical people just as I did in Bali. I remember flying in an anesthesiologist, a neurosurgeon, a chest surgeon, and other specialists from the military just in case they were needed. They would examine the local medical facilities and talk with their Icelandic opposite numbers, but generally just be there in case they were needed.

It was cold, rainy, and miserable during our two days in Reykjavík. Open-air bleachers across from the entrance to Hofti House where Reagan and Gorbachev were meeting were packed with many of the estimated 5,000 rain-soaked reporters and photographers from around the world who were covering the summit, including *U.S. News'* Nick Daniloff. Press people began slipping away in droves as hour after hour went by with no news. But sitting on the front row, with her pen and pad at the ready, was the UPI's indomitable Helen Thomas. Bill Henkle, the president's executive assistant, kept calling out to her from a second floor window in Hofti House, "Helen, it's nice and warm in here." "Helen, do you want to come in here and dry off?" She couldn't, of course, but I had to admire her professionalism for toughing it out just in case something should happen, while other reporters young enough to be her grandchildren were running for shelter.

I stayed with President Reagan at the home of the U.S. ambassador, who had moved out for the occasion. On my first night there, I had hoped to have a salmon for dinner taken from one of Iceland's ice-cold fjords. But what I got was a steak flown over from the White House. I did get my salmon later on, and the ambassador was thoughtful enough to give me a big frozen salmon steak as a gift to bring home.

We were no sooner back in Washington than I resumed my plans to return home to be with my critically ill brother and aged mother. But again fate intervened, this time in the form of medical problems with two of the three doctors who helped me look after Ronald Reagan, George Bush, and their wives.

Dr. John Hutton awoke one morning and found he couldn't get out of bed because of a horrible backache. He couldn't move, required sedation, and needed an ambulance to get him to Walter Reed Army Hospital. My first thought was that he might have some kind of malignancy, or maybe was going to be impaired and wouldn't be able to accompany the president on long trips, which are very arduous. You must be able to move fast, you can't stumble and fall, and backaches can be very demoralizing. It took another three weeks before I was convinced Dr. Hutton was getting better, and would be able to resume his duties and ultimately replace me.

Then Dr. Robert Gasser, our fourth doctor, fell to the ground and broke his arm while mountain climbing in West Virginia. As if that wasn't bad enough, a rock came tumbling down and struck him in the forehead. This knocked him unconscious, gave him a depressed fracture, and meant he had to be taken to a nearby private hospital for surgical correction. Dr. Gasser had lost quite a bit of blood, but refused blood transfusions because of his fear of getting AIDS. So we had to wait for his own blood supply to build back up, which takes time.

Dr. Hutton was now recovered, and I dispatched him to West Virginia to do what he could for Dr. Gasser. Dr. Hutton said Dr. Gasser was being well taken care of, but that we could not transfer him to a less costly military hospital because his doctors didn't want him to be moved. When we told Vice President Bush what had happened to Dr. Gasser, he and Mrs. Bush wanted to jump on a plane and fly out to see him even though I had told them he was unconscious and wouldn't know they were there (and that the winter weather and mountainous terrain surrounding the hospital made such a trip very risky). So I told them they just couldn't go, and although they were beside themselves, they did as I suggested.

It was a month before Dr. Gasser returned to work, which delayed my departure for home, as did November's revelations about the Reagan Administration's sale of arms to Iran and its support of the contra "freedom fighters" in Nicaragua. I kept looking for an opening, a peaches-and-cream time to tell President Reagan I was leaving—but I couldn't find one. I revised the date on my letter of resignation from August, to September, to October, and finally to November, by which time it was pretty tattered since I had been carrying it around in my pocket waiting for the right moment. The letter read:

THE WHITE HOUSE
Washington

November 1, 1986

My dear Mr. President,

> "They made me the keeper of the vineyards,
> but mine own vines have I not kept."

As the eldest son of my family, I am faced with impending responsibilities that cause me to believe I should return home to California. The current good condition of your health suggests that this is an ideal time to make possible an orderly transition for my successor.

I am most anxious to accommodate your schedule and your wishes in this matter. I will, of course, be pleased to make myself available for future consultations, or to assist in any way I can. As to my date of departure, after the first of the year might be an appropriate time. However, I will leave at your pleasure.

You have made it possible for me to share in a unique experience, for which I am extremely grateful. The example you have set with your tactful dedication to the challenge facing our great country, and your continued successes in finding solutions to those challenges, have earned my lasting admiration and will continue to be a source of inspiration.

Sincerely,
T. Burton Smith

It wasn't until Thanksgiving at the Reagan ranch that I managed to get the president alone. He had just unsaddled his horse, and we were walking back toward the house, when I said, "Mr. President, I think it's a good time now for me to depart because of my brother's worsening condition and my mother's getting older." "Well," he said in his familiar way, "you've got to do what you've got to do." And so Kit and I prepared to leave Washington to go home.

On December 4, 1986, the White House press office issued a statement to the media, which said:

The President has accepted with deep regret the resignation of T. Burton Smith, M.D., as Physician to the President, effective at a date to be determined. Dr. Smith spoke with the President at Rancho del Cielo last week and informed him of his desire to return to California to attend to pending family business. The President is deeply grateful to Dr. Smith for his loyal and dedicated service and for the great personal sacrifices he and Mrs. Smith made in moving to Washington. A successor to Dr. Smith will be named in the near future.

Six days later, I received this letter from President Reagan:

THE WHITE HOUSE
Washington

December 10, 1986

Dear Burton:

I wish there were a way to put in a few words how grateful I am for your service as Physician to the President, or how much Nancy and I will miss having you on our team at the White House. Perhaps it would be enough just to say that the past two years have been the best part of our very good friendship.

Nothing has impressed me more during my time in office than the willingness of so many talented people to put aside their own pursuits and to serve in the public interest. I am fortunate in a special way that you agreed to come east and take on this new responsibility. We've logged quite a few miles together, and you've even been asked to make some rounds on my behalf, but you and the fine staff under your supervision have always performed your jobs with true professionalism and a calm indifference to being in the public eye. One thing you certainly can't fault me for since you came on board is failing to keep you busy.

You have my heartfelt thanks and best wishes as you go to tend those vineyards of yours. Nancy and I are proud to have known you these many years, and you have our deep affection and respect. May you, Kathleen and the family enjoy every future happiness and success.

Sincerely,
Ron

My departure immediately brought up the question of my replacement, and I strongly recommended my chief of staff, Dr. John Hutton, who is an excellent surgeon the president knew personally. Larry Speakes put out a press release on December 10 saying Dr. Hutton was replacing me as physician to the president. This set off several days of press speculation as to the "real" reason I was leaving. Don Regan was under fire at this time and was about to resign as the president's chief of staff, and other reporters kept asking why everybody was suddenly jumping ship.

They were particularly curious about me because they knew I was a urologist, and an expert on the very kind of prostate surgery the president was scheduled to have some time after my departure. But I knew this was a routine operation. There was no cancer as far as we could tell (although anytime you remove what you think is a normal prostate there's a ten percent chance it will be malignant). It's also worth noting that cancer of the prostate rarely ever occurs before age fifty. But when a man hits fifty it goes up to a three percent chance, at sixty it's something like eleven percent, at seventy it's twenty-one percent, and at eighty you're up to thirty percent. That means nearly one out of three men is going to have prostate cancer at age eighty. But it can be a slow grower, and there are several good treatments available to help control—but not cure—this disease, if surgery is not possible.

I'm a great believer in annual physical checkups after fifty, but you don't need to have all the tests done every time—if your cholesterol's always been good, if your blood pressure's been good, if you have a good family history. You don't have to have things like an electrocardiogram, a chest X ray (because of the radiation risk), or a gallbladder check done every year. Your family physician can do these examinations, get good baseline data, and if something suspicious is found, the family physician can always send you to a specialist to have it examined in greater depth.

A few weeks before our departure on January 3, 1987, I began receiving mementos from many of those with whom I had worked during my two years in the White House. My staff gave me a desk clock inscribed "In Appreciation for Your Service to Our Country and the President." Marine Helicopter Squadron One gave me a photograph of the president's HMX1 helicopter. And there were certificates of appreciation from the Camp David staff and medical department, as well as the U.S. Secret Service.

One drawback to ending my two-year tour of duty at the White House during the Christmas–New Year holiday was that it's a dead time, when few people are around and very little gets done. President Reagan was at his California ranch, so Kit and I simply walked out of the White House alone. No champagne party with all our friends gathered around. No good-byes. Just an empty feeling as we closed the White House door behind us to resume our life in California.

Kit and I didn't want to start our drive back across the country because it was January, and not a particularly good time to travel. So we decided to take a two-week holiday in the Caribbean since I was now completely free for the first time in two years. We were West Coast people who didn't know too much about the Caribbean. But within a few hours after leaving a cold and icy Washington, D.C., we were reveling in its hot sunny weather, blue skies, and lush green islands. we spent a week on St. Thomas at Conejo Bay, sailed around for several more days, and then tied up for a final week on St. Croix before ending our most relaxing vacation in years.

We returned to Washington to say our last good-bye to President Reagan, who had invited Kit and me to the White House for a farewell meeting in the Oval Office at 3:45 P.M. on January 28, 1987. Jim Kuhn ushered us in to the president's small private inner office next to the Oval Office, but the president himself didn't appear until 3:52 P.M., full of apologies because his last appointment had run over and he hated to be late.

The president was scheduled to give a nationwide television talk in another eight minutes, yet he joined us at a small table and chatted with us as if we were the only two people in the world. Jim Kuhn kept looking at his watch, and when it got to be 3:58 P.M. he was visibly nervous, because by this time the president was engrossed in telling us about some lovely snow sculptures nature had built right outside his window. The president then rose from his chair, Kit and I stood up with him, and he gave her a going-away present of a beautiful commemorative plate, and me a pair of cuff links embossed with his signature and the presidential seal. He shook our hands, said a final good-bye, and strode toward the Oval Office a few feet away with only seconds to spare before he was due to go on the air.

President Reagan then gave me a presidential commission making me a member of the Board of Regents of the Uniformed Services University of the Health Sciences in Bethesda, Maryland, within walking distance of the Bethesda Naval Medical Center. Graduates of the university receive M.D. degrees and become captains in the Army or Air Force and lieutenants in the Public Health Service or the Navy.

The men and women selected are given room, board, uniforms, a modest salary, and a crackerjack medical education in return for spending another seven years in the service as doctors following graduation. The U.S. Senate had to confirm my appointment to the school's Board of Regents, which was held up for a year by the Iran-contra hearings and by yet another Secret Service investigation of my background.

My brother died on February 24, 1988, and a few days later I received a personal note of condolence from President Reagan. I received another one a week after my mother died on July 6, 1988, and it reminded me again of the unfailing thoughtfulness the president always showed toward those who knew him. His note on my mother's death read:

THE WHITE HOUSE
Washington

July 10, 1988

Dear Burton:

    Nancy and I were very sorry to learn of your mother's death. We know it must be particularly difficult for you to lose her so soon after the death of your brother.

    God blessed your mother with long life and your family with many years to enjoy her love and companionship. When Nancy's mother died last fall, we went through what you must be facing now, and what comforted us most was the knowledge that we were saying not a good-bye, but a temporary farewell to a woman who brought Nancy into this life and is waiting now with other loved ones to welcome us in the next. That part of our creed has sweetened our sorrow and made it easier to bear.

    We are keeping you and your family in our thoughts and we pray that peace and consolation will be yours. With our deepest sympathy.

Sincerely,
Ron

It was a weird, depressing experience to say good-bye to the president and end my days as his personal physician. Before, I could walk anywhere in the White House. I had carte blanche. People would greet me and say, "Hello, Dr. Smith." "How are you Dr. Smith?" Then suddenly I was outside the gate looking in. I was getting vacant stares from the guards. I knew I couldn't get in without an invitation. I still had my White House badge with its big black letters WHS—for "White House Staff"—which I always wore around my neck. But it was now stamped "VOID." My White House career was over.